Bamberg and Franconia

GERMANY'S BREWING HEARTLAND

A guide to Beers, Breweries and Pubs

SECOND EDITION

JOHN CONEN

TO JANE AND ALEX

Published by John Conen, 9 Scott Close, Farnham
Common, Buckinghamshire SL2 3HT, United Kingdom.

First Published 2003
Second Edition 2010

Printed and bound in the United Kingdom by
Lavenham Press, Lavenham, Suffolk

Book design: Dale Tomlinson (daletomlinson.com)
Typeface(s): Trilogy *by Jeremy Tankard* (typography.net)
Maps: John Macklin (johnmacklin.com)

ISBN 978-0-9544426-3-7

PICTURE CREDITS
Weyermann Speciality Malts 11
Steve Thomas 15, 44, 76, 90
Heller-Bräu Schlenkerla 22
Mike Rose 23
Christian Fiedler 24, 28, 29
Jim Kowalczyk 37
Ian Hasell 17, 18, 38, 40, 41, 49, 50, 53, 86
Chris Pollard & Siobhan McGinn 16, 20, 47, 54, 55, 64
All other photographs are by the author.
Cartoons by Marc Buchner 43

Great effort has gone into researching the contents of
this book, but no responsibility can be taken for errors.

Contents

ACKNOWLEDGEMENTS

Over the years many people have provided me with valuable assistance in researching this book. In particular, I should like to mention, in Bamberg, Gerhard Schoolmann of Abseits, Johannes Schulters and his colleagues at the Franconian Brewery Museum; Matthias Trum at Schlenkerla; Georg Wörner at Kaiserdom; Andy Gänstaller at Mahrsbräu; Sabine Weyermann of Weyermann Speciality Malts; Alexandra von Rohr and her staff at the Sprachtinstitut Treffpunkt, especially Martin Schippel; Anna-Maria Schühlein at the tourist office in Bamberg; Frank Wetzel; the Kalb family, who have always made me welcome at Fässla in Bamberg, and of course all the Bambergers who have shared their enthusiasm for their city's beer with me, and the brewmasters who took the time and trouble to show me their craft. I am also grateful to Oscar Maisel and Stefan Kolb of Gebr.Maisel, Bayreuth. Olaf Schellenberg, who has been instrumental in importing Franconian beers to the UK has enabled me to sample many of them without leaving the country. I should also like to thank my colleagues in CAMRA, the Campaign for Real Ale who have given me invaluable help and feedback from their visits to the region; Dave Cunningham, for allowing me to consult his private translations of various German books on beer; Martin Beavon for translating other articles and correspondence for me; Steve Heathman for putting my guide on the web; Bob Thompson who shared his research in the region, particularly with regard to Zoigl pubs; Ian and Jill Hasell, Jos Brouwer, John White and Fred Waltman also provided information and advice. Ian Townsend and Paul Denny gave valuable assistance with the photographs. Finally I should like to thank Mark Webb for his invaluable guidance in publishing this book.

I am grateful to the Bamberg Tourist Office, the various Bamberg breweries and Weyermann maltings for providing photographs and other reference material for this book.

ACKNOWLEDGEMENTS for the 2nd Edition, 2010

I am grateful to CAMRA for their help in marketing both editions of this book. I continue to be indebted to beer lovers who give me more information and assistance. The contributors to the Online Beer Guide to Bamberg and Franconia website in particular are a source of valuable first-hand information on the changing local brewing scene. Thanks go to Ian Hasell, Mike Rose, Jim Kowalczyk, Chris Pollard, Christian Fiedler, Steve Thomas, Heller-Bräu Schlenkerla and Weyermann Specialty Malts who provided photographs for this edition. I am also grateful to Marc Buchner for his permission to use some of his wonderful cartoons in this edition. Finally, Lieselotte Tomaschek gave me invaluable help with translations and information on *Dialekt*.

Introduction
Bamberg, the miracle city

THIS IS A GUIDE both for beer lovers and for visitors. Back in 1983, an article by Graham Lees in CAMRA's *What's Brewing* newspaper described the delights of the Franconian brewing tradition and briefly mentioned Bamberg's ten breweries and smoke beer. Appetites whetted, a CAMRA colleague and I were soon on our way to Bamberg. There was no detailed information in the article nor was there at that time any published information that could have helped two beer British lovers arriving in this city. So on arrival we had to resort to the good old Yellow Pages and the street map to track down the breweries and their outlets. Helpfully, the Klosterbräu brewery was depicted in a photograph accompanying the article; we tried to find it by looking for the church towering behind it (the Stephanskirche), only to find that there was no brewery tap, an omission since remedied. The information we gleaned on this trip formed the basis of my first beer guide to the city.

Since 1983 I have visited this splendid city many times. Many other beer enthusiasts find their way here too, no doubt drawn, as I am, to distinctive, full-flavoured beers, pubs as close in character to British pubs as any one would find in Europe and an enthusiastic, dedicated local following for the beer. For Bambergers love their beer. The popularity of the traditional taverns such as Fässla, Spezial and Schlenkerla testifies to this, as does the mass exodus to the beer gardens or Kellers in fine weather. About ten years ago, statistics showed that beer consumption per head was 220 litres per annum in Bavaria compared to 146 litres per annum for West Germany as a whole. Bamberg capped these with an impressive 330 litres per capita! This has no doubt reduced in recent years but the proportions remain constant.

This book is the product of the many enjoyable visits I have made to Bamberg. Fortunately, change is not a feature of pubs and beers in Franconia, although ongoing closures of breweries continue to be a concern to all lovers of the local brewing tradition.

For two reasons, Bamberg is a miracle city. Firstly, its escape from obliteration by bombing in the Second World War, the fate of so many German cities. Its architecture reflects 1000 years of history and delights visitors with baroque churches, renaissance palaces, and solid merchant houses. Bamberg is built on seven hills, like Rome and Sheffield. Rome cannot match Bamberg's brewing tradition, but a native of Sheffield might find some parallels with the steel city's drinking traditions. Bamberg's seven hills are the Kaulberg, Domberg, Jakobsberg, Altenberg, Michaelsberg, Abtsberg and Stephansberg, the latter known as the "Kellerberg" because it is the location of several of Bamberg's famous beer gardens. This hilly profile means there are unrivalled vistas of the timbered houses, cobbled streets and tiled roofs of the old city, and the honey-coloured sandstone and slate roofs of the ecclesiastical buildings.

The second miracle is the survival of its brewing tradition with its nine breweries, traditional taverns and local dedication to a unique beer culture. Bamberg is in fact the centre of the Franconian brewing industry – there are breweries in many of the towns and villages in the river valleys around the city, with over 150 breweries within a 35-kilometre radius. Most of these are simple brewpubs, located in small villages most visitors will never have heard of. They mainly brew for their own customers although about half of them also distribute their beers over a small area to other pubs and to the local drinks market. But most brew less than 10,000 hectolitres a year, which in British terms equates to about 6,000 barrels. This is comparable with some of the new British microbreweries. There are also a number of larger breweries, brewing up to 150,000 hl per annum, and even these are located in relatively small towns, brewing up to 150,000 hl per annum. Further afield there are large breweries in Nuremberg, Kulmbach and Bayreuth that are amongst Bavaria's largest producers of beer.

The approach to Bamberg by rail from Nuremberg heightens the anticipation with a view of the traditional but alas defunct Maisel brewery east of the railway and the vast Weyermann maltings by the station. Bamberg station and its surroundings are not a very promising introduction to the city, but you soon leave the 21st century behind, and by cutting through the 17th century streets of the old market gardening quarter, you will soon sight the chimney at the rear of the Fässla brewery, and start your exploration of Bamberg's brewing heritage.

Bamberg is outstanding even in Germany for its excellent selection of beers. Of the nine breweries operating, five are effectively brew-pubs, and two of the nine produce the famous local speciality, smoke beer (Rauchbier). Even if Rauchbier is not to your taste you can choose between over 50 beers brewed in the city. There are many more beers available in the city supplied by the numerous breweries in neighbouring towns and villages.

This book is primarily for beer lovers but will hopefully appeal to all visitors. Please read on for more information on how to enjoy the miracle that is Bamberg.

Notes to the Second Edition, 2010

It is appropriate here to pay a tribute to two people who died in 2007, both of whom did much to further interest in the beers of Bamberg and Franconia. Michael Jackson, the internationally renowned beer writer was one of the first British beer writers to explore the area in the 1970s and became an inspiration to all those who followed. John White devoted his retirement to the cause of European beer, and collected and disseminated a huge amount of valuable information. He also led several "beer hunts" to Bamberg to introduce British beer lovers to the delights of Franconian beer, food and culture. His website www.whitebeertravels.co.uk is maintained in his memory.

The Franconian brewing tradition

The dawn of consumerism?

Bamberg lies in the heart of Franconia, a region that still boasts nearly three hundred breweries, which must be the biggest concentration of breweries in the world. This is where ancient brewing traditions survive, with a pub and brewery business often combined with farming and other activities. Unlike Britain, virtually all breweries have their own pub, but as in Britain the smaller breweries are under threat. Many family-run pub and brewery businesses suffered from under-investment, problems of succession and a dwindling local market for their products. Some ceased brewing and sold out to larger brewers. Those who are more enterprising are now benefiting from a nation-wide revival of interest in traditional brewing styles and are enjoying an expanding distribution area following the reunification of Germany. But the problem of succession – the availability and willingness of a heir to take on a very heavy workload – is still a very real one in Franconian breweries today.

Over 100 breweries have closed in the last twenty years and this is a disturbing trend, even if recently, the rate of closures has slowed. Whilst Franconians are enthusiastic about their native beers, there is more than a little evidence that they do not realise how fortunate they are to have such a strong tradition still in place. They are surprised at the interest shown by British visitors who have a consumer body in CAMRA to protect their interests. However, it must be said that sterling work has been done by the professional brewers of the region to promote the local brewing traditions. For example, they have organised "beer days" and "beer seminars" in Bamberg, there are "beer routes" directing tourists to small breweries, and several excellent museums of brewing have been established. There is a hint of "nostalgia" in some of this action, as there was in the early days of CAMRA in Britain. But this all has to be seen in the context of Germany as a whole where there is little evidence of any consumer movement emerging and the lack of critical writing on beer is surprising given Germany's high profile as a beer-drinking nation. A plus for future campaigning is that local consumers are well informed about beer, far more so than in the UK, and hopefully opportunities will arise for the local consumer to play a positive role in the preservation of the local brewing heritage.

Consideration of the future of medium and large sized breweries of Franconia has also to be made in a wider context. The German brewing industry, although dedicated to purity and freshness of the product, is generally seen as very conservative. Comparisons have been made to the British brewing industry of 40 or so years ago, before brewing passed out of the hands of the old brewing dynasties into the hands of multi-nationals. This has started to happen in Germany – the consolidation that has taken place in such a major brewing centre as Kulmbach is a worrying example within Franconia itself.

Criticism has even been levied at Germany's Reinheitsgebot, the purity law which stipulates that beer can only be made from hops, malted barley, water and yeast. How can this be wrong you may ask? It's simple – pure ingredients alone do not necessarily guarantee a superb finished product. The Reinheitsgebot permits no sugar, spices, fruit, unmalted cereals or cereals other than barley to be used in brewing (there is a special amendment to cover wheat beers). This means a German brewer cannot attempt the more exotic beers brewed in Belgium and the UK, or at least cannot call them beer if he does! However this does not excuse the disappointingly unadventurous beer offering of draught Export or Pils (or often just Pils) which is standard throughout much of Germany.

By contrast, in Franconia you will find a superb range of traditional beers, brewed within the Reinheitsgebot and putting much of the rest of Germany to shame.

Local beer specialities

1· **Vollbier**. "Full beer" is an official categorisation of German beer of a certain strength, but in Franconia it is used by brewers to describe their standard beer. According to the writers Hollhüber and Kaul, Vollbier should traditionally be a darkish red-gold colour and be relatively strongly hopped, with a palate balancing a fine bitterness with a malty sweetness. They claim that Vollbier can actually vary from light gold in the sandstone landscape of the Steigerwald to the South-West of Bamberg where the brewing water is soft, to almost black in colour in the region known as "Franconian Switzerland" where the brewing water from the chalk landscape is very hard.

2· **"Ungespundet" Lagerbier or Kellerbier**. This is often brewed as an alternative to a Vollbier. "Ungespundet" means literally "unbunged". Until recent times, lagering of beer took place in wooden vessels, which were basically large barrels. These had a vent or bunghole (Spundloch) in the top, the bung or tap (Spund) for which was usually partially

opened early in the lagering process, to prevent the build up of carbon dioxide causing the vessel to burst!

Nowadays, beers are lagered in stainless steel vessels with a pressure valve that controls the amount of carbonation in the beer. Therefore most lager beers are now "gespundet". The term "ungespundet" still indicates that the beer has been lagered or matured with most of its carbon dioxide escaping to the atmosphere, hence its low carbon dioxide content (kohlensäurearme). Because of its high hop rate, its low carbonation and lack of filtration, coupled with the fact it is usually dispensed without carbon dioxide gas, this beer is pretty close in palate to a real draught British bitter.

There is no need for the British beer lover to shy away from the word "lager" which is simply the German word for "store". Although the British public equates "lager" to European beer, the word is largely unknown in Europe and even in Germany it is usually only used in the trade as a generic name for a beer that has been stored (i.e. most German beers). It's not usually used in the public arena and a request for a lager in a pub is likely to bring a blank response. The only exception is in the traditional brewing areas of Franconia where the term Lagerbier is still used. In Germany Lagerbier was used to describe the new bottom-fermented beers introduced in the nineteenth century to oust the old top fermented brews that were unstable and inconsistent. The new brews could be lagered or stored for use in the summer months after being brewed in the spring, hence their name. The brewing traditions of the nineteenth century still survive in Franconia. The move to paler beers in the 1920s bypassed rural Franconia and after the war, partition of Germany and the closing of the Czech border added to its isolation. The term Lagerbier therefore is still commonly used.

Today the Franconian "ungespundete" Lagerbier or Kellerbier still retains the characteristics of those nineteenth century brews, although elsewhere in Germany the more modern, paler styles have long since taken over. In order to preserve it, it is relatively strongly hopped and it is less malty than Vollbier. It is unfiltered with a slight yeast haze. Finally, it will usually be dispensed straight from the wooden barrel, without carbon dioxide pressure, into ceramic mugs. It is refreshing and ideal for drinking outside on a sunny day. The name Kellerbier reflects the link with the Kellers, the traditional Franconian beer gardens established where this beer was lagered in cool underground "cellars".

Not all breweries in Franconia actually brew a Kellerbier; two of the most distinctive local Kellerbiers are brewed in Buttenheim, a small town that supports two medium sized breweries, St.Georgen and Löwenbräu. To complicate matters there are lagerbiers that are not ungespundet (for example at the Fässla in Bamberg), and Vollbiers that are unfiltered!

3 · **Bockbier**. Bockbier is said to derive its name from the city of Einbeck, where it originated. It is also the German name for a billy goat and this animal is often depicted on Bockbier labels and advertisements. It is similar to a brewery's Vollbier, but substantially stronger. Bamberg's Bockbier season begins around Mid-October and lasts until Christmas and most of the local breweries produce a Bock at this time, which are available for varying lengths of time – Schlenkerla's Bock for example is available until early January. The season starts with Schlenkerla's Bock in mid-October, followed by Klosterbräu, Mahrs and Fässla later in the month, Spezial in early November and the short (two-week) season of Greifenklau in Mid-November. Celebrations mark the tapping of the first Bock of the season, for example at Klosterbräu, and the Kellers may even open. Some breweries also follow the Bavarian tradition of a strong beer (Doppelbock) for Lent and a further Bockbier in May, and the Beck brewery at Trabelsdorf has even produced a Triple Bock!

4 · **Festbier**. Again similar to Vollbier, but only a little stronger, produced for Christmas (Weinachtsbier) or for other religious festivals and Kerwa. See also Märzen below.

5 · **Pils**. The popularity of Pils has swept from the North West across the whole of Germany and now it seems that no brewery can afford not to brew it. The characteristic dryish, hoppy flavour of pilsener style beer is not always evident in the Pils style beers produced by the smaller Franconian breweries.

6 · **Rauchbier (smoke beer)**. Rauchbier is the speciality that has made Bamberg famous. The flavour of this beer is achieved by kilning the malt over a beechwood fire. In a memorable description, the writer Oz Clarke, was enthused: "rich malt, bitter hops and the skins of Virginia hams smoked on the hearth – a sensational beer". At the other end of the spectrum, it has been less flatteringly dubbed as "liquid kippers"! Rauchbier is accurately translated as "smoke beer" rather than "smoked beer" as it is the malt it is brewed from that is smoked, not the beer itself. I've found misleading definitions published – for example that the taste of Rauchbier "comes from being filtered through charred beechwood logs" and in another source that it was created accidentally when a monastery brewery caught fire! Rauchbier has been regarded as a style of its own and a Bamberg speciality since before the Second World War. This was not always the case – in the early days of malting, all malt was kilned over wood fires and thus all beers would have had a more or less smoky aroma. This continued until coal became cheap in the nineteenth century and maltings switched to coke-fired kilns, which were also suited to the production of pale malt for the increasingly fashionable paler beers. It is said that even in Britain darker beers continued to be made from smoked malts until well into this century. In Franconia the main fuel was beechwood from the vast forests of the region and remained a cost-effective alternative to coal for smaller breweries with their own maltings.

In 1936 four Bamberg breweries still produced Rauchbier but today Schlenkerla and Spezial are the only true examples of the tradition. They produce their own malt and brew mainly Rauchbier, an immensely popular beer both in their pubs and as a guest beer in others. Other Franconian breweries have revived Rauchbier production in recent years to enhance their range of local beers.

7 · **Märzen**. The name derives from the month of March (März in German) which was the last opportunity to brew beer before the hot summer weather set in and made the brewing process risky. The beer was traditionally tapped in the autumn at such events as Munich's Oktoberfest. In Franconia, Festbiers are Märzen-type beers but the term is also used for a stronger than average beer that is available at all times. Schlenkerla Rauchbier, for example, is described as being of Märzen strength.

8 · **Schwarzbier**. Bamberg always had its own "little black beer" in Klosterbräu's Schwärzla, but black beer is becoming popular nationally following the discovery of East Germany's Köstritzer Schwarzbier after the reunification of Germany. Others are now following the style. It's not really black in colour, just a very dark lager beer. Although the darkest malts are used, you won't find any use of roasted barley, which is so characteristic of British stouts and porter.

9 · **Weissbier (wheat beer)**. Wheat beer is a very ancient, top-fermenting beer style predating bottom-fermented lagers, and had almost died out when a revival began in the 1970s. As Pils has invaded Franconia from the North, Weissbier has spread up from Southern Bavaria and is finding its way into the portfolios of most breweries in Franconia. Weissbier (literally "white" beer) is the name used locally in preference to Weizenbier (wheat beer). Wheat beer must be brewed from at least 50% wheat malt. Weissbier is usually available in sedimented form (Hefe-Weissbier) and is served in tall distinctive glasses that emphasise its characteristic foaming head. Generally available only in bottles, although some draught versions are available e.g. from Mahrs and Kaiserdom.

As a "family" of beers Weissbier can appear in pale and dark versions at standard strength and also at Bock and Doppelbock strength. Occasionally you can find a "Kristall" or filtered version, but like the Bock and Doppelbock versions, this is more common in Munich and Southern Bavaria.

1998 will be remembered as the year when something of a mini wheat beer revolution came to Bamberg. The Schlenkerla, Spezial, Fässla and Keesman breweries all introduced new bottled wheat beers, Fässla having both pale and dark varieties: those who know this brewery will not be surprised that they were named "Weizla"! The wheat beers from Schlenkerla and Spezial naturally employ smoked malt in addition to wheat malt, with fascinating results. Kaiserdom and Mahrs have brewed wheat beers for some time, the latter producing an excellent dark Weisse Bock (7.2% ABV) for Lent. However, at least some of the new wheat beers were contract brewed by non-Bamberg breweries. The now defunct Maisel produced Bamberg's first wheat beer and got into trouble with their namesake in Bayreuth who already brewed Maisel's Weisse; they pointedly re-named it Eine Bamberger Weisse! On my recent visits Weissbier still doesn't seem to be very widely drunk in Bamberg but no doubt it now has its niche and will not fade away like the low alcohol beers of the early nineties.

10 · **Other beers**. Franconian brewers are happy to call their beer simply "Lager" or "Vollbier" and do not usually bother with fancy names! But there are a number of local beers which do not fall into the above categories; they often represent attempts to resurrect beer styles of the nineteen twenties or earlier, before paler coloured beers began to predominate. Names such as Bauernbier (farmer's beer), Landbier (country beer), Braunbier (brown beer) and Alt Fränkisch (old Franconian) are used to lend authenticity. Zwickelbier usually refers to an unfiltered lager, and is similar to a Kellerbier, although it may not have its characteristic low carbonation.

Rauchenfels Steinbier was a revival of an ancient technique using white-hot stones in the production of the beer; it took place at the Rauchenfels brewery near Coburg. This brewery has now been closed and production of the beer transferred to a site near Augsburg in Bavaria. Dampfbier or steam beer is a top-fermented speciality produced by the Maisel brewery in Bayreuth. Malzbier is a black malt drink, completely non-alcoholic.

Malt and hops are God's gifts

A brewing centre like Bamberg is naturally also a centre of malting, and has two large malting companies. The Weyermann maltings is a local landmark and its red-brick building, surmounted by chimneys with the distinctive local cowls, seems to ride like a steamship at anchor across the railway tracks from Bamberg station. This massive building is a superb example of industrial architecture and is a protected historic monument. About 50% of Weyermann's production goes for export, to over 67 countries including the US, Canada and Japan where its wide range of "speciality malts" is in demand by creative brewers, particularly in the fast-growing microbrewery sector. Weyermann also proudly claimed that

it is Bamberg's 10th brewery – it produces SINAMA,® a roasted malt beer extract brewed according to the Reinheitsgebot and concentrated in a vacuum evaporator. This claim has been given more substance as Weyermann now has a pilot brewery where creative international brewers can experiment to their hearts' content with Weyermann® malts in a 2.5 hl Kaspar Schulz mono-bloc brew house. Pure malt extract is also produced for use by microbreweries and home brewers. Weyermann was founded in 1879 by Johann Baptist Weyermann, a grain merchant, and today its president is Sabine Weyermann, the fourth generation of the family. The excellent website with English option is at **www.weyermann.de**.

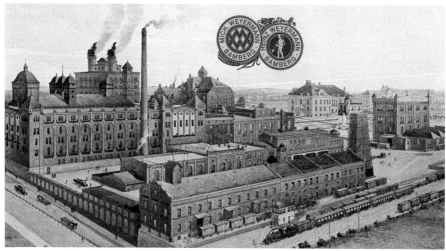

The Weyermann maltings in 1929, and (top right) a recent aerial photograph.

Bamberg's other major maltster is the Bamberger Mälzerei in south Bamberg, founded in 1889 www.bamberger-maelzerei.de.

Bamberg is also conveniently close to two of Germany's premier hop-growing areas, the Spalt and Hersbruck regions near Nuremberg. Christian Fiedler tells us that Bamberg itself was for a while a hop-growing area. Originally, Bamberg brewers preferred Bohemian hops, Franconian hops being regarded as inferior. However, during the 19th century hop cultivation increased significantly in the Bamberg area and, Bamberg developed into one of the most important trade locations for hops in Germany after Nuremberg. Hop gardens became part of the scenery on the hills of Bamberg. From 1892 poor harvests and growing competitive pressure from abroad ended the boom in hop cultivation, and the remaining cultivated land was given up in the 1930s.

No account of Bamberg's brewing industry would be complete without a mention of the firm of Kaspar Schulz, equipment makers for over 200 years, who have supplied and installed equipment for breweries all over the region, and indeed all over the world www.kaspar-schulz.com.

Strength of beers

Stammwürze is the term used by German brewers to denote the original strength of the brewing wort prior to fermentation, and expresses the fermentable solids of the brew in degrees Plato. This is similar to the expression of "original gravity" in British beers. However, German bottle and cask labels usually give the percentage of alcohol by volume (ABV) of the beer, although this is rarely shown on menus or price lists in pubs.

German beers are officially classified by Stammwürze into:

(a) **Schankbier**, which equates to British "low alcohol" beer and has a Stammwürze of between 7 and 11. This results in beers with up to 3.5% alcohol by volume (ABV). In the early 1990s some breweries introduced light (Leicht) beers which fall into this category – most seemed to have disappeared again fairly quickly!

(b) **Vollbier**, i.e. full (strength) beer. Most German beers fall into this category and have a Stammwürze of between 11 and 14 and an ABV of 3.5 to 5.5% ABV. Märzen and Festbier are slightly stronger (Stammwürze 13 to 16).

(c) **Starkbier**. Strong beer, for example Bock and Doppelbock, with a Stammwürze of at least 16, giving an ABV of 6.5% or more.

The strength of individual beers may vary slightly depending on the particular brew. It is safe to say that most beers in Franconia are around the 5% ABV mark, with Bockbier usually having an ABV of 6 to 6.5% and the much rarer Doppelbocks an ABV of 7% or more.

Alcohol free beer (Alkoholfreies Bier) will have a Stammwürze under 7 and less than 0.5% alcohol.

Packaging and dispense of beer

Most Franconian brewers supply their draught beer in casks, made from wood, aluminium or a compound with a wooden effect, with two apertures, one to let air in and the other to let the beer out. There the similarity to British Real Ale or cask conditioned beer ends, as Franconian beer, in common with all bottom-fermented "lager" beer is sent out ready to serve with no need for the beer to settle or condition further in the pub. The concept of draught beer undergoing further conditioning in casks in the pub cellar is unknown in Germany. Some Franconian lagers are unfiltered or only roughly filtered, but are nevertheless intended to be served this way i.e. with a certain yeast cloudiness.

A variety of dispense systems is used, but it is often possible to find beer dispensed straight from the barrel. The term "ohne Kohlen-säureanstich" denotes that carbon dioxide gas is not used in dispense. Dispense direct from the barrel (known as Bavarian dispense or "Bayerisches Anstich") increasingly tends only to be used only on special occasions, for example at festivals, and it's now less common in Bamberg although some pubs, including Schlenkerla and Mahrs, still retain it. Small brewpubs and Kellers in the countryside often use gravity dispense. For outlets where turnover is slow, draught beer is filled into kegs for pressure dispense, as filtered beer can soon lose condition and warm up. Sizes of cask range from 10 litres up to 100 litres. Some brewpubs now serve the beer direct from tanks.

Bottled versions of beers are generally identical to the draught, undergoing exactly the same processes before being filled into bottles, and may be offered in preference to tapping a new barrel of draught near closing time. Breweries do not normally make much of the distinction between draught and bottled beers and most beers produced are available in both formats. Pubs tend to have the most popular beers, which naturally have the highest turnover, on draught.

Because it is brewed only from malt, hops and yeast, and because greater care is taken in dispense, draught beers in Germany tend to be less gassy and more flavoursome than British keg beers and lagers.

All draught beer is served with a generous head into a lined glass allowing a good head through which to drink the beer – at least 3cm in depth. The British style of serving "lager" in brim measure glasses with virtually no head would be totally unacceptable any-where in Germany. The principle here is that the gas in the beer is used to form the head, leaving the beer itself far less gassy than is the practice in Britain. It is reckoned that it should take 5/7 minutes to dispense a glass of Pils – you will see pubs conscientiously filling a num-ber of glasses simultaneously, by a topping up system in which the head is allowed to subside before a further shot of beer is added from the tap. This system is applied to all draught beers in some pubs. Unfortunately some pubs indulge in rapid dispense of draught beer, leaving the beer too gassy, but with dispense straight from the barrel there is far less chance of this happening.

Bottom-fermented lager beers should be stored and served at 7–9 degrees Celsius. Subtle differences in taste can be detected with differences in temperatures but bottom fermented beers do not taste as pleasant if served at similar temperatures to British ales. About 8 degrees Celsius is also the correct temperature for serving German top-fermented beers such as Weissbier.

For most of the year, weather conditions in Franconia are more or less similar to Britain (Franconia in fact inclines to a more extreme "continental" climate with severe winters) and bring the same problems in that temperatures can vary widely on a daily and a seasonal basis. This means that on some occasions draught beer may be a little cold, particularly for British tastes, given the weather conditions and ambient temperature. Some pubs have little electric immersion heaters or other devices for warming up your beer, though it is only the elderly or those with weak stomachs that are reckoned to avail themselves of this service.

Bottled beers almost without exception come in half litre bottles, crown capped and in cases of 20. Bottles are either of the short stumpy "Euro" variety or the taller "NRW" variety that is now gradually replacing them. "Flip top" bottles are enjoying a limited resurrection as a marketing ploy, ironically they were almost standard in this region only 50 or 60 years ago. Bottled beers from the smaller breweries are likely to be unpasteurised and have a limited shelf life. This of course limits their marketability except in outlets with a high turnover. Traditional pubs have no problem but modern cafes and bars and supermarkets may.

In "green" Germany, recycling of bottles is very important and empties are always returned to the point of sale. Only a very small proportion of local output of beer goes into one trip bottles and cans.

Brewery output is usually given in hecto-litres (100 litres) which equate to 22 UK gallons or 26 US gallons.

Measures

A half-litre is the usual measure for draught beer in Bamberg and Franconia and is known as a "Seidla" although this technically refers to a glass without a handle. You will find this type of glass in Keesman and Schlenkerla, but a heavy, handled mug (Henkel) is also used, as in Greifenklau, Spezial and Fässla. Pils type beers may be served in a glass with a stem. Local breweries produce plenty of attractive glasses and ceramic mugs, a wide variety of which can be purchased at the gift shop Manger at its branches near Schlenkerla in central Bamberg. Ceramic mugs, called Steinkrug or Krug but never "Stein", are usually found in the Kellers and beergardens, where they help to keep beer cool in hot weather. You might like to acquire a Bierkellerdäggala, which is a wooden lid designed to keep the wasps out of your mug of beer!

Unlike in Munich and southern Bavaria, litre measures are the exception rather than the rule in Franconian beergardens. Franconians tend to consume more beer with less fuss than the macho Bavarians of Munich! The traditional pubs serve half litres as standard. If you don't want a half-litre, you could share a beer. When you order your final beer of the session you might be content to order a "Schnitt" which is an unmeasured quarter litre of beer in a half litre glass – if you're lucky, more. Don't abuse this by ordering a "Schnitt" as your first beer of the evening, or by ordering more than one! Some pubs do not serve a "Schnitt" at all. More upmarket pubs may have smaller measures on offer, for example 25, 33 or 40 centilitres for those who want a small beer.

DRINKING FRANCONIAN BEERS BACK HOME

It is difficult to find beers from Bamberg and Franconia outside Germany. Besides the fact that most are produced in small, family-run breweries, without the facilities to export beer, the beers are usually unpasteurised and have a short shelf life. This does not lend them to commercial export in bulk. However, thanks to the efforts of a few specialist importers, they can be found in a limited number of beer shops and pubs in the UK and elsewhere, and for the last 15 years or so, enjoyed at several of CAMRA's beer festivals. They also make some well-received appearances at beer festivals and other events across Europe.

See the website www.germanbeerguide.co.uk for details of UK shops and restaurants stocking German beers.

www.biermarkt.com is a Bamberg website offering online purchase of Franconian beers. Beer can of course be purchased at low prices at all Franconian breweries and there are in addition some drinks warehouses in the Bamberg area where you can choose from a wide range of local beers.

www.realbeer.com will offer help to USA drinkers.

Bamberg's breweries:
their history and traditions

Further information on the breweries' tied pubs (Gaststätte) and other outlets, including opening times and directions, can be found from page 36. See the map on pages 92–3 for locations.

Ambräusianum

Dominikanerstraße 10, Bamberg 96052
T 0951 5090262
www.ambraeusianum.de

BEERS: **Hell**, **Dunkel** and **Bernsteinweizen** (amber wheat beer), and a **Doppelbock** for the autumn Bock season. Ambräusianum brews are only available on draught and are only sold in the pub.

Although rumours about a new brew pub opening were common in the 1980s and 1990s, one can only admire the enterprise or audacity of anyone who actually succeeded in opening a new "brew pub" in Bamberg! Ambräusianum opened in August 2004 and was Bamberg's first new brewery since 1961, and restored the total of breweries in Bamberg to 10 for the first time since the closure of Lowenbrau in 1991. It claims to be the first and only brew pub in Bamberg and it is indeed the only example in the city of the modern "brew pub" which now appears all over the world and has the brewing equipment as a centrepiece in the bar. The equipment is a 10HL Kaspar Schulz kit that previously did service in a Berlin brewpub. The brewing process can be viewed and the date of the next brew is displayed in the bar.

The pub occupies the Haus Mahr, two doors down from Schlenkerla, and the the business is run by Ambros Mahr, whose family have owned the building since 1809. The building is a former palace of the Counts of Schrottenberg and dates back to 1267. It was previously a restaurant called the Altes Hofreit, and prior to that the Hofbräu-Schänke, a tap for the eponymous brewery that closed in 1977.

Fässla

Ob. Königstraße 19/21, 96052 Bamberg
T 26516   FAX 201989
www.faessla.de

BEERS: **Lagerbier, Gold-Pils, Zwergla, Weizla, Bambergator**.

Königstraße had no fewer than 23 breweries at the beginning of the 19th century. The breweries were attracted here because it was part of an old trade route, the former Steinweg [Stone Way], the importance of which can be seen in its being named as a paved carriage-way. Merchants and other travellers brought good business to the brewers, who as a rule also offered their customers overnight accommodation and stabling for the horses. With the building of mass transport systems the Steinweg lost the importance that had grown over centuries: The Ludwig-Donau-Main canal and the connection of Bamberg to the railway network displaced the stream of goods and accelerated the decline of the breweries. Of the 23 breweries recorded in 1817, only Fässla and Spezial have survived until today.

Originally the site of Fässla was a feudal tenure of the religious foundation of St. Gangolf and is mentioned as such as early as 1398. The property did not acquire a brewery until two and a half centuries later when in 1649, a cooper called Johann Kauer acquired it. This was just after the end of the Thirty Years' War,

when trade began to revive after the traumatic effects of that conflict locally. The business remained in the ownership of the family for the next two generations; after various changes in ownership over the years, a cooper from Bischberg called Anton Kröner became the brewery owner in the "Fässchen". At this time the brewery output peaked at a very modest output of 363 hl per year. Anton Kröner suffered considerable loss when a fire destroyed the brewery and pub in 1818. Later the ruins were taken over by Andreas Kramer and rebuilt again, thus creating the building we see today.

In May 1824 a journeyman brewer called Heinrich Leicht acquired the newly erected building. The substantial purchase sum of 7,400 Gulden for the pub and brewery certainly came from the inheritance left by his father, the former owner of the Karmeliterbräu. On 20 January 1898 the brewer Paul Lutz took over the "Fässchen". Under his 26-year management he established the brewery among the medium sized businesses of Bamberg. His first large investment involved the deepening of the ice cellar on the Oberer Stephansberg, where he ran a small beer garden in the summer. With luck and fortune Paul Lutz steered his brewery through the madness of the First World War, before his unexpected death at the age of 53. The brewing operation was nevertheless maintained since on 17 April 1926 his daughter married Friedrich Zehender, who came from Gleisenau. Together they ran the business through the difficult time of the Second World War. When Friedrich Zehender died in 1951 his widow Maria together with her sister Gretel ran the brewery until into old age.

On 1 April 1978 the brewery – then still called Fässchen – was rented to master brewer and maltster Sebastian Kalb, At that time the brewery's output was about 2,400 hl a year. After a tenancy of over eight years Herr Kalb purchased the entire brewery property in 1986. After taking over the business the Kalb family invested millions of Deutschmarks to restore the building, re-equip the brewery and upgrade the guest accommodation.

The Brauerei Fässla and its "dwarf" trade-mark typifies the old Franconian pub business, combining pub, restaurant and hotel; Fässla is however one of those that chooses to look forward and capitalise on its traditional assets and now, more than 350 years after it was founded, the "Fässla" is very much a modern business. The investment carried out has enabled the annual beer output to rise to 16,000 hl. Sebastian Kalb's son Roland now heads up the business.

The traditional style Lagerbier and Pils are popular on draught in the pub and there is also a Märzen beer called Zwergla (little dwarf) after the brewery's trade mark, and the newer pale and dark wheat beers (Weizla), all in bottles. A few years ago all the beers except Weizla were increased in strength. In the Bock beer season, Bambergator, Bamberg's strong-est beer (8.5% ABV), makes a triumphant appearance. The ending "-ator" is a Bavarian tradition – not normally followed in Franconia, for naming a seasonal Doppelbock. There are a number of other pubs in the Bamberg area selling Fässla beer, and there is the usual take-out and home delivery service.

Greifenklau

Laurenziplatz 20, 96049 Bamberg
T 53219   FAX 59599
www.greifenklau.de

BEERS: **Lagerbier**, **Weizen**, **Bock**.

The actual history of the brewery starts at the beginning of the 18th century when Franz Friedrich von Greifenklau, acquired several properties on the Kaulberg. He had a tavern and brewery built, including a barn, stable, hall and *Hofreit*, His coat of arms depicts a griffin's claw. After his death the business passed through many hands. In the early 1900s husband and wife Andreas and Anna Bergbauer ran the Greifenklau brewery, but they received several complaints from the city authorities on account of hygiene deficiencies. That led eventually to the situation at the beginning of 1914 that beer could only be sold as off-sales while the pub had to remain shut. In the same year the brewery property was compulsorily auctioned and it was acquired by Sigmund Brockard. The whole establishment must have been in a desolate state, because the new owner had to have his beer brewed in the Riegelhof brewery until 1919. Not until then was the brewery ready for operation.

Greifenklau, which is now in the fourth generation of the Brockard family, was Bam-berg's smallest brewery until Ambräusianum opened, producing 1200HL per annum, most

Keesmann

Wunderburg 5, 96050 Bamberg
T 9819810   FAX 9819814
www.keesmann-braeu.de

BEERS: **Herren-Pils**, **Helles**, **Sternla**, **Weissbier**, **Bock**, **Josephi-Bock**.

Wunderburg is a village that has now been swallowed up in Bamberg's suburbia. The history surrounding the "wonder" that gave its name to the village is not clear but the presence of two brewpubs here is wonderful in itself. The building was in the ownership of the Keesmann family before its foundation as a brewery in 1867. From the 1960s onwards the brewery and pub were extensively modernised.

Keesmann's flagship beer is the "Gentlemen's Pils" (Herren-Pils), first brewed in 1979. There is also a Helles and in recent years Sternla, a traditional ungespundetes Lagerbier has been brewed. Since the spring of 2003 there has also been the "Josephi-Bock", a Lenten Bock available from the middle of March until the end of April. There is also a pale Bock for the traditional Autumn Bock season.

Keesmann beer is very popular around the Bamberg region and can be found in several pubs and at local festivals.

of which is sold on draught in Greifenklau's own pub and beergarden. The brewery, rebuilt in the 1950s, produces a pale lagerbier, called simply Lagerbier or Greifenklaubier. In the 1930s Greifenklau was a Rauchbier brewery but today we are told that any apparent smokiness in today's beer is not due to the use of Rauchmalt. A Weizenbier and a Bock beer are also brewed, the latter appearing for a short season in November.

Greifenklau owns a modern hotel, the Altenburgblick (**T** 95310) which is situated behind the pub, down a steep hill, in the street called Panzerleite. The Laurenzikerwa, the festival of the nearby chapel of St. Laurence, takes place on the second weekend of August in the streets adjacent to Greifenklau.

Kaiserdom

Breitäckerstraße 9, 96049 Bamberg
T 60450   FAX 604560
www.kaiserdom.de

BEERS: **Extra-Dry Pils, Alt-Bamberg Dunkel, Meranier** (Schwarzbier), **Weizenland Hefeweissbier**, and others.

The largest brewery in Bamberg, brewing in a modern plant situated behind the old brewery buildings of Burgerbräu in the suburb of Gaustadt. It has been in the ownership of the Wörner family since 1718. In 1986 the brewery ambitiously rebadged itself as Kaiserdom, which is the name given to Bamberg's Cathedral, and projects a much more modern image than the other Bamberg breweries. The brewery itself is totally modern and employs the latest brewing technology.

Kaiserdom produces around 180,000 hectolitres of beer every year and in its portfolio are beers for export all over the world, including non-alcoholic beer for Saudi Arabia and kosher beer for Israel. Kaiserdom also produce soft drinks and alcopops, and contract brews and packages beers for other companies. Kaiserdom beer is also produced under licence in Sweden and China. Prostel, a non-alcoholic beer is widely available locally.

Kaiserdom beers can be drunk in many pubs in Bamberg, including the Kaiserdom-Brauereigasthof & hotel, in Gaustadt itself. In the city of Bamberg there is the Rathausschenke, the quaint little mediaeval pub on the old bridge over the Regnitz, the extensive restoration of which was completed by Kaiserdom in 1997.

Klosterbräu

Ob. Mühlbrücke 3, 96049 Bamberg
T 52265   FAX 500274
www.klosterbraeu.de

BEERS: **Gold Pils, Schwärzla, Braunbier, Bockbier, Maibock, Schwärzla-Bock, Braun's Weisse**.

Klosterbräu has been brewing for over 450 years in its picturesque riverside brewery, one of Bamberg's oldest timber-framed buildings, and a splendid sight when viewed from across the river. Kloster is German for monastery, but despite the name this is a secular brewery, first documented in 1333 and established as the Brown Beer House of Bamberg's Prince-Bishops (the city's religious rulers) in 1533; it brewed for them until 1790 when it passed into private hands. It has been in the ownership of the Braun family since 1851. You would not guess that in more recent times, there was for many years no brewery tap on the site, and the current facilities have been developed since June 1988. The beer range was expanded along traditional lines but in recent years the range has been cut back. There is plenty of interesting breweriana (as well as beer) for sale at the brewery's shop on the corner of Judenstrasse. Klosterbräu produces a brochure in English, and there is a good website.

Mahr's Bräu

Wunderburg 10, 96050 Bamberg
T 915170   FAX 9151730
www.mahrs.de

BEERS: **Vollbier**, **Pils**, **Ungespundete Lagerbier**
(popularly known as "U"), **Bockbier**, **Mahrs-Weisse**,
Weisse Bock, **Gig**.

One of two breweries in the suburb of Wunderburg, the present name of this brewery goes back to the acquisition by Karl Mahr in 1840. The purchase agreement included the property "known as the Ziegelhütte, together with a rear building, a granary, stables, a garden house, a well, a brewery, a *Witzgarten*, skittle

alley and yard space". In 1868 Karl Mahr acquired a hillside cellar site on the Oberer Stephansberg and ran the summer beer garden "Zum Brenner-Keller" above. It is the site of today's numbers 34–38, which is still in the ownership of the brewery today as the "Mahrs-Keller". In 1897 the ice cellar was expanded to a capacity of about 1,000 cubic metres and was cooled with natural ice until 1954. In 1960 the hillside cellar lost its importance as a cool cellar, and three years later the beer garden was closed. The "Mahrs-Keller" was not opened again until 1986, after a fundamental renovation.

From 1889 Andreas Burkard ran the brewery. He was married to Agathe Michel and in 1885 he took advantage of the opportunity to take over the Weiße Taube brewery on Zinkenwörth in the centre of Bamberg. Thereupon he sold the property in Wunderburg to his brother-in-law Johann Michel junior. Since that time the Mahrs brewery has been in the possession of the Michel family.

The 17th century building houses a pub of great character, behind which is the early 20th century brew house, now completely modernised. Nevertheless, production is still on a small enough scale to ensure distinctive beers, and Mahrs has an impressive range, including the popular "U" or ungespundetes Lagerbier. A seasonal pale Bock beer is tapped in October, and at Lent, an unusual dark Weisse Bock, introduced in 1992, appears. Gig doesn't have any connection with rock concerts – it's a dark Märzenbier beer, named after the horse and trap once used by the Michels to make deliveries to customers.

Mahrs has a small distillery that produces a Bierschnapps and a range of liqueurs made from local fruit. The Mahrs website is very good (mainly in German), and gives full details of the beers and other information. Mahrs supply many pubs in the Bamberg area including of course the Mahrs Keller which also still belongs to the Michel family.

Schlenkerla
(Heller-Bräu Trum)

Dominikanerstraße 6, 96049 Bamberg
T 56060   FAX 54019 (office)
Obere Stephansberg 27–31, 96049 Bamberg
(brewery)
www.schlenkerla.de

BEERS: **Aecht Schlenkerla Rauchbier, Urbock, Helles Lagerbier, Weissbier.**

Founded in 1678, the Brauerei Heller produces the most famous of Bamberg's beers, Aecht Schlenkerla Rauchbier, and serves it in the equally famous brewery tap in Dominikanerstraße. The official foundation date of Schlenkerla is 1678, but brewing probably took place here much at a much earlier date. Previous buildings on this site were destroyed in the Thirty Years' War. In the 18th century the brewery was owned by the Heller family and from them comes the current formal name of today's brewery, "Heller-Bräu" Trum. In 1872 the Graser family acquired the brewery, and the name Schlenkerla takes its name from the German verb schlenkern, to walk with a shambling gait, and is a reference to Andreas Graser who had a disability, though it is now known that this was probably a result of an accident rather than drinking his own beer! He is depicted on the brewery's bottle labels and caps.

Under the Trum family – Elizabeth Graser married Jakob Trum who later became brewmaster in 1936 – Schlenkerla has been developed into a modern business but with its roots firmly in tradition. It operates on firmly traditional lines, but with a modern emphasis on quality which is achieved by controlling all the stages of production from malting through to dispense of the finished product. The brewery still has its own maltings to produce the special smoked malt, kilned over local beechwood. The beer is widely available in Bamberg.
In the 19th century lagering facilities on the Stephansberg were acquired. This was the brewery's "Keller" where the beer was lagered in cool cellar caves in the hillside during the hot summer months. There was also a beer garden here but this closed at the time of the First

World War and never reopened, and the site is now given over entirely to brewing. The beer is still lagered in those original sandstone caves.

In 1935 the brewing operation was transferred to the Stephansberg, although the malting process remained at Dominikanerstraße until 1971. The brewery on the Stephanberg was rebuilt after further land was acquired on the corner of Sternwartstraße. The beers are distributed across Germany, and their fame now extends around the world. Today's brewery remains in the hands of the Trum family, Matthias Trum, a graduate of the Weihenstephan School of brewing, having taken over the business from his parents in 2003.

The pub has also been expanded over the years, today's kitchens and toilets occupying the part of the premises previously used for

21

Spezial

Ob. Königstraße 10, 96052 Bamberg
T 24304   FAX 26330
www.brauerei-spezial.de

BEERS: **Lagerbier, Märzen, Ungespundete, Weizen, Bock**.

The Spezial brewery is not only one of the most beautiful breweries in Bamberg, it is also one of the most traditional. The property in Obere Königstraße still has the appearance of a typical brewing operation from the 16th century. On the ground floor the front building houses a pub, above which are overnight accommodation and the living accommodation of the owning family. A broad carriageway through the yard forms the entrance to the pub rooms, to the take-away servery or *Schenke* and to the rear part of the property. There the brew house is located, separated by a small yard. According to an inscription this was built in 1742. As hundreds of years ago, today too the brewing barley is malted, giving the "Spezial-Bier" its typical smoky taste. Only the stables formerly used for draught animals are no longer used.

As early as 1357 the property is mentioned as in the ownership of a *Pfister* called Fritz Bischof. But the building, which is listed as a protected monument, with its wonderful half-timbered facade, dates from the 15th century and could already have had today's appearance when a brew of beer was first made in it. The founder of the brewery is considered to be a cooper Linhard Großkopf, whose family owned other breweries in the Steinweg about 1536. How the brewery got its name is uncertain. Although this brewery-guesthouse is indeed special, the name could derive from "Spezeln" a local dialect word for a gathering of friends. Other sources suggest it appears for the first time in connection with Niklas Delscher who "was called Spical, was a brewer and also a cooper". He ran the brewery from 1631 until his death on 5 April 1664. The brewery has been owned by the Merz family since 1898.

The brewery also supplies a few other local outlets in addition to the popular beergarden (the Spezi Keller) on the Stephansberg. Spezial

brewing and malting. In the 1930s the Grasers leased the neighbouring building, formerly part of a Dominican priory, from the Bavarian government. This was converted into a bar and a separate function room. A more recent addition is the beer garden, in the area next to the pub, which was used by the University as a car park, and in the past only used by Schlenkerla at Sandkerwa and for the Bockbier tapping. It is now open from Easter until October.

Schlenkerla has a good website (German and English) which includes details of the production of Rauchbier.

In addition to the distinctive Rauchbier, Schlenkerla brew a "Helles Lagerbier" which is not a Rauchbier but nevertheless picks up a hint of smoke from the brewery's yeast. It is not available in the Schlenkerla pub. The Weissbier, available only in bottles, presents an amazing combination of fruity wheat and smoky flavours. Fastenbeer is a regular beer every Lent and is served from Ash Wednesday to Easter. It is unfiltered and made from a blend of Rauchmalz and pale malt, and is only available on draught in the pub.

In 2009 a new Christmas Doppelbock was introduced: Schlenkerla Eiche or Oak Smoke. Its malts are kilned with oakwood instead of beechwood, and hence it has a totally different smoky character to the classic Schlenkerla.

brews a range of smoke beers (the brewery has its own tiny maltings) and in addition to the draught Rauchbier, there is also bottled Märzen and Weizen, and a seasonal Bock. They provide an interesting contrast to the more overtly smoky beers of Schlenkerla. An ungespundete Lagerbier, first introduced a few years ago, appears in spring and autumn, but is not a Rauchbier.

The story of the breweries of Bamberg in the 20th century

The Bamberg "beer war"

How important *"ihr Seidla Bier"* ["your mug of beer"] is to the people of Bamberg was shown in 1907. The local breweries unanimously decided that from 1 October that year they would increase the price of beer from 11 to 12 Pfennigs and they would no longer serve the *Nachbier ("Heislein")* or "near beer" for one Pfennig per half litre. The Bamberg population was shocked at such a drastic measure since the phrase "beer price increase" did not exist in Bamberg speech – the last increase in the price of beer had actually been 110 years earlier – in 1797, by the prince bishop's government. The normally apathetic citizenry of Bamberg rapidly united and boycotted the beer of the local breweries – the well-known Bamberg beer war had broken out. Under the strategic leadership of "Field Marshal" Karl Panzer, two pubs – "Mondschein" and "Weierich" – served beer from Forchheim and so circumvented the profiteering prices of the local breweries. At first the master brewers wanted to sit out the crisis, but as more and more horse drawn drays with barrels of beer headed from Forchheim to Bamberg they gave up their resistance. On 7 October they withdrew the increase in the beer price and thus ended the people's boycott. Nevertheless the beer war had consequences: Ludwig Rübsam, the chairman of the Bären- und Eckenbüttnerbräu brewery lost his position as chairman of the Bamberg Brewery Association [*Bamberger Brauverein*]. Members blamed him for having been responsible for promoting the price increase.

In the early 19th century Bamberg had over 60 breweries and it was probably at this time that it could be claimed that Bamberg had more breweries than churches. By 1908 only 38 remained. During the 20th century, breweries continued to close, the First World War in particular having a disastrous impact, and by 1941 when Victor Zobel wrote about his "blissful beer travel" around Bamberg, only nineteen were operating. Since then eleven of the breweries he described have gone (he didn't include Burgerbräu, today's Kaiserdom, in the suburb of Gaustadt). This is a depressing saga, which will be all too familiar to beer lovers in all countries with long brewing traditions.

The first major impact of the Second World War came at the beginning of 1940, when a law was enacted whereby the original gravity of German beer was not to exceed 10.3 percent. The purpose of this measure was to save 500,000 tonnes of barley annually, which was needed for other use (processed foods, *ersatz* coffee and animal fodder). In the following years the shortage of raw materials and energy led to the closure of many breweries.

The second major impact came from air raids. Although Bamberg was one of the few cities of Germany not to suffer major destruction in the Second World War, it did not escape entirely and in the closing months of the war serious damage was done by Allied bombing and shelling. Fortunately most of the major monuments and landmarks escaped damage but over 300 buildings were totally destroyed. including three of Bamberg's breweries – Kleebaum, Kaiserwirt and Wilde Rose.

Kleebaum Brewery

Kleebaum

The Kleebaum brewery, situated at Untere Kaulberg 7 near to the Obere Pfarrkirche, was totally destroyed in the air raid which took place about 13:00 on the afternoon of February 22 1945. This brewpub dated back at least to the middle of the 18th century and occupied a fine building with a beautiful Baroque frontage.

Kaiserwirt and the Doppel brewery

The Doppel brewery is notable because it was the last brewery to be founded in Bamberg before Ambräusianum opened in 2003. Its founder, Lorenz Doppel, came from the long-established Bamberg brewing family of Dotterweich, which ran the Kaiserwirt brewery for many generations. The last owner of the Kaiserwirt was Lorenz Doppel's elder brother Richard. Brewing in the Kaiserwirt ended on 13 April 1945 when the pub and brewery on the Mittlerer Kaulberg (no. 11) were severely

damaged by artillery fire as Allied forces entered Bamberg. As Richard Doppel was suffering ill-health, the brewery was never rebuilt, but the pub continued to be run by the family until 1974, taking beer from the Polarbär- und Blaulöwenbräu. Since 1978 the building has no longer been a pub. The "Kaiserwirts-Keller" also suffered serious damage through an American air raid. According to Christian Fiedler, Richard Doppel's daughter, Käthe Haag, still remembers 22 February 1945, when at about one o'clock in the afternoon the bombs hit the kitchen building and "the dumplings rolled onto the ground"!

Lorenz Doppel qualified as a brewer at Weihenstephan in 1936 and ran a small country brewery in Schney near Lichtenfels until he was called up for war service. After his return he rented the Einhorn brewery in the Sandstraße in Bamberg (this had ceased

THE LOST LOCAL

A Dr Schneidmadl mourned the loss of Kleebaum in an article in the Bamberg Yearbook in 1950:

"First of all the splendid hosts, the passionate hunter and violin player Franz Müller and his genial wife Margarete deserve an appreciation. One, a tremendous manifestation of the art of winning hearts, the other an upright citizen's plump and comely wife – both live on in my memory. They were people of the old school, held in high esteem, who had respect for tradition but nevertheless were not shut off from new practicalities. To see this, you only had to go into the spick and span, panelled kitchen in the courtyard, where I often took away roasts of venison, deer and rabbit. I also took out from the *Schenke* the requisite *Mass* of "ungespundenes", that all Bamberg's "Bierkiesers" were keen on. When "ungespundenes" was served, the potbellies of Bamberg did not bother to make the ascent of the Kaulberg and the pub with the original windows on the courtyard was overcrowded.

I have been told that as a schoolboy at the turn of the century I was a regular but naturally only at the "Gassenschenke" (serving counter on the street), where every two days I had to collect three half litres. Evening after evening I leapt or skipped, whistling, with a pot-bellied glass mug to Röckelein or Kleebaum, where the "double" and "single" beers were already tapped – a litre of "double" formerly for 24 Pfennigs, later for 26 Pfennigs - the landlord then filled my mug full with "double" from his copper jug.

Mind you, the locals would not go for "single" beer. Asking for anything other than "double" would have been an offence. But the landlord of the Kleebaum had another requirement which was an affront to the Bamberg beer drinker, "När sich kan Schlappgroschn gem!" is a well-known saying of Bamberg people,* and means "don't be shown up for not having enough money".

As the faster child I was always early and had to wait for the time-consuming procedure of tapping the barrels, in Summer the barrels were kept in the cellar, in the cooler Spring and Autumn they stood in the entrance hall, and in severe Winter they waited for tapping in a circle around the old fashioned tall "cannon" stove. The full barrels came thundering in from the entrance hall through a little doorway under the shelf of the *Schenke*, which was fitted with a brass plate and shone with polish and cleanliness. The empty barrels were rolled out in the reverse direction and piled up in the hall. Here also stood one or two of the typical Bamberg beer wagons. The barrels, the stables, the kitchen and the brewery mixed together in an indescribable aroma that I can still smell today. I never experienced quarrels, brawls or stabbings in this genuine, well-run brewpub.

In the single large bar – there was no Nebenzimmer – stood great tables with polished maple tops. The bar had three windows overlooking the street, which were as long as I could remember hung with old grey shutters. During the day one couldn't see out of the dark bar so curtains were superfluous. Naturally each guest had a tin-lidded beer mug that belonged to this distinguished brewery. The beer mats were top quality felt and not poor quality cardboard. Next to the bar was an armchair for the licensee's wife, so she could keep an eye on proceedings, and this completed the cosy interior of the room.

*This saying is no longer current in Bamberg. Translating it proved a challenging experience!

Nearly everybody played *Schafkopf* (literally: sheep's head), the most popular Bamberg card-game."

Franz Müller died in 1939 and his son Rudolf took over the business. In 1943 brewing had to cease because of the exigencies of war. Dr. Schneidmadl, who as an adult had remained a regular at Kleebaum, completes the story:

"I could not have foreseen that simple pleasures in this pub were soon to cease, in the last months before the catastrophe I played card games or chatted at the *Stammtisch* of the gardeners. My diary for 21 January 1945 reads "evening drink at the Kleebaum. The little barrels were returned under the *Schenke* to the hall. The simple shutters, the iron stove with its long chimney, the scrubbed maplewood tables and four parties of *Schafkopf* made me feel at home. I talked about the good old days with friends of my father, the coachman Müller (88) and the cidermaker Scharnagel (72)." One month later, smoke arose from a tall heap of rubble. Today, five years after the destruction still nothing is standing of this ancient Bamberg place of joyful living. The gable end on the narrow Kleebaumgasse stares to the heavens. One prays for the resurrection of this vanished, hospitable brewery refuge."

Shortly afterwards, Dr. Schneidmadl's prayers were in part answered and a temporary pub was erected in the ruins, run by Rudolf Müller's wife Eva. But Kleebaum never brewed again. Following a fire in 1977 the pub was demolished and an apartment block now occupies the site. I am grateful for the assistance given by my friends in Bamberg in translating this article. The wonderful book *Bamberg – Die wahre Haupstadt des Bieres* by Christian Fiedler filled in gaps in the story.

brewing in 1944 due to the war), and its associated hillside Keller on the Jakobsberg. In 1950 he started brewing again and five years later he bought the entire property from Edmund Schlegel. The beer mats and mugs from that period bear the legend "Brauerei Lorenz Doppel und Einhornbräu".

Cramped conditions in the Sandstraße premises and obsolete brewery equipment were not conducive to a modern brewing operation and eventually Herr Doppel built a completely new brewery building at Oberer Kaulberg 39 next to the "Kaiserwirts-Keller", which was still in the ownership of the Doppel family.

With the provision of the new building in 1961, the brewery at Einhorn closed and the "Brauerei Doppel" came into existence. About the same time the last three of the brewery's horse-drawn drays were taken out of service. At its peak the business had three outlets of its own in Bamberg – "Kaiserwirts-Keller", "Ahörnla" [local dialect for "Einhorn"] and the "Einhorn-Keller", which were supplied with *Märzen*, *Bock* and *Pils*. In addition a *Festbier* was produced for special occasions. A small fleet of vehicles supplied customers throughout Upper and Lower Franconia and even delivered to Frankfurt am Main.

Not quite ten years after the new building was completed, the imminent closure of the operation was announced. The management decided not to produce their own beer any more but to contract out production to other firms. Henceforth *Rauchbier* was taken from the Spezial brewery and *Pils* from Bamberger Hofbräu AG. This was followed in 1971 by the final closure of the business and the sale of the warehouse to Hacker-Pschorr-Bräu AG of Munich. The brewery was converted into apartments between 1973 and 1976, but is still clearly a brewery!

The former "Kaiserwirts-Keller" on Oberer Kaulberg 37 was used by the brewery only as a summer beer garden. I understand that it now only opens once a year for the local church festival, the Laurenzi-Kerwa. But when I visited the festival in 2002, the Keller was only serving wine! Nearby you can still see a Hacker-Pschorr

advertisement on a wall. The Einhorn pub survives but in recent years has traded under the name "Nelson Lounge", and the small Einhorn-Keller, which dates back to the fifteenth century, is still open on the Jakobsberg. Both still sell Hacker-Pschorr beer.

Wilde Rose

The brewing tradition at Wilde Rose in Keßlerstraße went back to 1628. In 1794 Johann Kauer, the brewing master at "Zur Rose", acquired a barn with a hillside cellar on the top of the Stephansberg, which in the following period he expanded several times. In the middle of the 19th century the beer garden was opened and in 1873 a large music pavilion was built. The beer garden was closed from 1941 until 1971.

On 22 February 1945, the Wilde Rose brewery and the pub in Keßlerstraße were razed to the ground in an air raid, and rebuilding was not completed until 1953. The range of beers at this time included a *Märzenbier* "Wilde Rose Gold" as well as a *Vollbier*, a *Pilsener* and a *Bockbier*. In January 1967 Johann Konrad passed the business over to his son Arnulf. Four years later he ceased brewing. In the same year efforts started to reopen the large beer garden on the Oberer Stephansberg, which had been closed to the public since 1941. Today the "Wilde Rose-Keller" is still run by the Konrad family. Although beer was supplied by Kaiser of Neuhaus-Pegnitz for many years, from 1996 the customers were able to enjoy beer produced by a Bamberg brewery, the Wilde Rose beers being brewed by Maisel.

Even for those breweries that had not suffered damage in the air raids of 1945, the post-war years were not easy. In October 1945 the American command in the Frankfurt headquarters prohibited brewing by Bavarian breweries. In the subsequent period this order was relaxed. From 24 April 1948 the breweries could officially produce a beer substitute drink that could be sold against bread coupons. And in December 1949 permission was given for a *Vollbier* of 11 to 14 percent original gravity to be brewed. The currency reform of June

1949 ended the regulation of the market and beer production soon resumed in full swing.

In the 1950s, 1960s and 1970s another nine breweries closed. Mostly the reason why the business was not continued was lack of investment or the lack of a successor. Only rarely was it lack of business acumen on the part of the owner. Mohrenpeter closed in 1947 and Riegelhof in 1953, when the owners and brewmasters retired.

Ringlein
Ceased brewing in 1957, but has remained in operation as a hotel and restaurant (see page 36). In the 1980s the property was extensively modernised and expanded with a hotel complex with its own underground car park. In the course of this, the old brew house was demolished. There was a Keller at Stephansberg 45.

Löwenbräu
The Blauer Löwe brewery originated at Judenstraße 2 and probably was in existence as early as 1472. In the late 19th century Wilhelm Nathan built a modern brewery on the Stephansberg, and brewing ceased at Judenstraße. By the 1930s the brewery was suffering financial difficulties and by 1934 was bankrupt. The owner of the Polar Bär brewery, the entrepreneurial Rudolph Diebitsch, bought Blau-Löwenbräu in March 1935 as part of his ambition to establish a large brewery enterprise, and henceforth he led the new undertaking under the name of "Polarbär- und Blaulöwenbräu". In 1936 Rudolf Diebitsch relocated the entire beer production into the brick building on Oberer Stephansberg 40. Henceforth this was also the head office of the merged businesses. Brewing ceased at Polarbär and the premises at Judenstraße were sold.

The start of the Second World War meant a sudden turning point for the aspiring brewing operation. In the late summer of 1939 the beer garden (the Polarbärenkeller) at Stephansberg 12 & 14, famous for its wonderful view, had to be closed. In the air raids of early 1945, the buildings at the Polarbärenkeller were destroyed.

After the death of Rudolph Diebitsch's widow Christine in 1965 the brewery came under new ownership as Bamberger Löwenbräu. Later Löwenbräu was sold to the Fecher brewery of Seligenstadt. The owners were offered a new site at Kramersfeld by the Bamberg authorities so that it could stay open, however they did not take up this offer, preferring to realise the value of the property, and the brewery closed in 1990 and was converted into apartments. The original Polar Bär in Judenstraße became the Bolero, a Spanish restaurant, in 1999, thus ending a tradition going back to 1675, when the owner was a gentleman named Pankraz (Pohla in local dialect) Behr.

Michaelsberg
The brewery on the Michaelsberg was the oldest brewery in the city. It has its origin in the brewery in the Benedictine monastery founded in 1008. The first proof of brewing by the monks is found in 1122. Like nearly all the monasteries of Bamberg the Benedictines farmed a large area and for their own use they also cultivated barley, wheat and hops. The beer they brewed was not only for their own use but was also used as a means of payment. In the course of secularisation the Benedictine monastery was dissolved in 1804 and passed over to the Citizens' Hospital Foundation [Bürgerspitalstiftung]. In contrast to many monastic breweries, however, the brewery was retained and henceforth it was leased to various brewers. In October 1899 the era of the Peßler family started, which saw the modernisation of the brewery. This popular brewery on the Michaelsberg came to a tragic end when Michael Peßler died on 13 January 1968, and, only three months later, his half brother Georg died. Michael Peßler's widow Anni Peßler with her daughter Anneliese tried to keep the brewing operation going, but a few months later they gave up thus ending brewing on the Michaelsberg after 850 years. The city of Bamberg then rented the pub to Maisel, who henceforth produced the "St. Michaelsberg" beers at their brewery in Moosstraße as a reminder of the centuries old tradition of the

View of Michaelsberg

former monastic brewery. The Franconian Brewery Museum was set up in the old brewery in 1984. The pub closed in 2003 although it later reopened as an Italian restaurant. The loss of this traditional pub and its pleasant little beer garden was a great blow.

Bamberger Hofbräu

For many years this was Bamberg's biggest brewery. Established in 1885 as the Erste Bamberger Exportbierbrauerei Frankenbräu, its buildings were situated in the Pödeldorferstraße. Amongst the Bamberg breweries, Hofbräu has a special position. In contrast to almost all the other local breweries it did not stem from a traditional craft business but was designed for industrial beer production from the beginning, like the Kulmbach breweries. In the 1970s together with other large brewer-

ies the Hofbräu AG became incorporated into the newly founded Patrizierbräu AG. It was believed that with the creation of a north Bavarian brewing group the intense competition then being felt in the brewing industry would be better withstood. However declining sales and the pressure of rising costs soon forced the head office in Nürnberg to make severe cuts. The brewery in Bamberg was also affected by the subsequent closures. At the end of 1977 Patrizierbräu AG gave up production on the Bamberg site. For a few years more beer with the label "Bamberger Hofbräu" was brewed by the sister company Humbser-Geismann AG in Fürth. Patrizier was taken over by Pschorrbräu in 1992. Just under a hundred years after their foundation, the Hofbräu brewery buildings were demolished.

Röckelein

The origin of the Röckelein brewery on Untere Kaulberg goes back to the 16th century. Johann Papsthart, acquired the brewery in 1892 and it remained in his family until closure. The brewery was badly damaged in an air raid on 22 February 1945, which destroyed the neighbouring Kleebaum brewery. In the course of rebuilding Hanns Papsthart, brother of the brewmaster Peter Papsthart, modernised the building and undertook numerous alterations. In addition a new brewery was built at the Keller site and the brewing operation was moved from the Unterer Kaulberg to Laurenzistraße. When Hanns Papsthart retired in 1968 the brewery was given up because there was no successor, and the property was sold to Löwenbräu of Munich. The original pub and brewery at Untere Kaulberg 36 is now the Tapas Cantina Bar Terrazza, after many years as the Domterrassen (it has a wonderful view of the cathedral from its terrace). Röckeleins-Keller at the summit of the Kaulberg, where the new brewhouse was built in the 1950s, was closed for redevelopment as housing a few years ago. The former brewhouse, complete with its brewing copper, remained in place until then.

Fortunately, the predatory inclinations of the big Munich and Nuremberg breweries, which were very evident at one time, do not seem to have had a lasting effect on today's pub scene. Bambergers like their native beers and tend to be hostile towards large non-Bamberg breweries, although the beers of the smaller Franconian country breweries are well-loved. The happy impression throughout this region is that a large number of small breweries continue to supply pubs with an enviable range of beers.

Maisel

Maisel, the second-largest brewery in Bamberg, had been on the risk list for many years and has now suffered the fate of so many medium-sized German breweries. The company went into liquidation in May 2008 and brewing ceased in August of that year. The brewery building is to be converted into apartments. The pubs owned by the brewery are still open: the Fässla brewery has bought the brewery tap, the Maisel Keller, which is now renamed the Fässla-Keller.

The large range of beers brewed by Maisel included an excellent Kellerbier in addition to the St. Michaelsberger Dunkel, Bamberger Hell, Pilsener, Festbier, Heller Bock, Dunkler Bock, Domreiter Pilsner, St. Michaelsberger Feinherben, St. Michaelsberger Urtyp, Kellerbier, and Eine Bamberger Weisse. Over 250 pubs in the region were supplied.

Founded in 1894, Privatbrauerei Maisel was an "industrial" brewery standing in a prominent position near the railway line to Nürnberg. In 1894 Rudolf Maisel acquired the Brauerei Sperber and its pub in Obere Königstraße and built a lagerkeller in Moosstraße. Initially, until the new brewery was built, the beer was transported to Moosstraße by horse-drawn drays for lagering. At this time there was a family connection with Maisel in Bayreuth, but in recent times the Bamberg brewery was no longer owned by the Maisel family.

The Franconian Brewery Museum

Fränkisches Brauereimuseum
Michaelsberg 10f, 96049 Bamberg
T 53016   FAX 52540
www.brauereimuseum.org

The Franconian Brewery Museum or
Fränkische Brauereimuseum (FBM) was set
up by a group of professional brewers in 1984
"out of love for the brewing tradition".
It occupies the renovated historical vaults
of the former Benedictine Abbey on the
Michaelsberg in Bamberg, where brewing
took place as early as 1122. Besides historical
equipment acquired from local breweries,
maltings and equipment manufacturers,
there are displays covering the whole of the
malting and brewing processes. There is
an amazing display of "Heath Robinson"
equipment that was at one time (but not that
long ago!) used to fill barrels and bottles,
and clean the same. Nostalgia abounds with
memorabilia in the form of advertisements,
beer glasses, mugs and mats from long-closed
breweries. There is an "ice cellar" where in
pre-refrigeration days, ice from the River
Regnitz was stored to keep the beer cool in
summer. A must for all visitors, and not only
beer lovers, because this is a very fine
museum indeed.

Every year the FBM hold a Nostalgie-Fest,
a kind of mini beer festival, and produce a
commemorative beer mug. In 2009 the FBM
celebrated its 30th anniversary with a beer
specially created at the Weyermann pilot
brewery. It was a Doppelbock called
Benediktator, brewed to a recipe from the
old Michaelsberg brewery.

The museum is open from April to
End October, 1300 to 1700, Wednesday to
Sundays. Parties can visit by appointment
at other times and an English-speaking
guide can be arranged. There is a small
admission charge.

Over 400 beer lovers support the
Franconian Brewery Museum by
subscribing as friends.

The European Beer Consumers Union (EBCU)

In 1993 UNESCO (United Nations Educational, Scientific and Cultural Organization) declared Bamberg to be a World Heritage City. On November 14th 2002 the EBCU (European Beer Consumers Union) declared Bamberg to be a World Beer Heritage City.

The European Beer Consumers' Union (FBCU) was formed in Bruges in May 1990 by CAMRA, the Campaign for Real Ale, of Great Britain, Objectieve Bier Proevers of Belgium and PINT of the Netherlands.

The three founding members have since been joined by similarly-minded national consumer groups from Austria, Czech Republic, Denmark, Finland, France, Italy, Norway, Poland, Sweden, Switzerland, and in Belgium, Zythos has taken the place of Objectieve Bierproevers which was wound up in 2002.

EBCU is a non-political, non-religious organisation formed to co-ordinate the European activities of the European National Beer consumer organisations. EBCU is totally independent, as are its constituent parts, of any outside control by brewery or other vested interests. Delegates from the 13 member organisations of EBCU meet twice a year to discuss policy, exchange information and identify campaigns to improve the lot of the beer drinker and pub-goer in Europe. EBCU also organizes regular receptions in Brussels for members of the European Parliament and the Commission.

EBCU is open to all non-exclusive national organisations of beer lovers which are independent of all outside influence, represent the beer consumer and can wholeheartedly endorse the following Aims ands Objectives. EBCU is formed to take whatever steps it feels necessary, by lobbying, advertising, publishing or whatever, to campaign for the widest possible support for these Four Aims and Objectives.

The Aims and Objectives of the EBCU:

Preservation of European Beer Culture
The preservation and maintenance of the European Beer culture, with particular regard to traditional, national, regional and local breweries, and traditional brewing beers.

Promotion of Traditional Beers
The promotion and support of all European breweries producing high quality traditional beer by traditional methods in accordance with established national and regional variations in style.

Support of Traditional Breweries
To campaign against any activities likely to lead to further concentration of control in the European brewing industry.

Representation of Beer Drinkers
To represent European drinkers in the campaign for choice, quality and value for money in beers and brewing.

Despite maintaining numerous contacts with numerous interested persons in Germany for more than a decade, EBCU does not currently have a German member organisation in its ranks. So far, German beer consumers seem to have failed to organise in reaction to the numerous acquisitions by multinational and closures that have occurred over the years. We hope this situation will eventually change and an independent and national beer consumers' organisation will be started in Germany to try and save what can still be saved of its wealth of beer traditions, beer styles, local breweries and drinking places.

Contact: **terry.lock@ebcu.org** or see website **www.ebcu.org** for contacts in member organisations.

Where to drink

Local pubs – the special atmosphere of the Gaststätte

Franconia's fine old taverns are amongst the best in Germany. Often housed in attractive old buildings, they have long and interesting histories, in some cases having flourished for centuries. Gaststätte is the most common name in these parts for a pub providing good food and drink, and perhaps accommodation as well. British drinkers will recognise all the attributes of good pubs; not only are they free of music and other distractions, they are usually true centres of the local community. The best are of course still home to a brewery.

At a typical Gaststätte, such as Fässla or Spezial in Bamberg, you enter through a stone archway with massive wooden doors opening into the courtyard (Hof). Immediately the era of horsedrawn traffic is conjured up, and this was in fact where the drays would have entered and left the brewery and where the draymen would have enjoyed a few beers. The "Schenke", a little serving hatch, enables customers to order a beer and later truthfully claim that they haven't been in the pub! This stand-up drinking area is called the "Schwemm" and customers will also collect cases and barrels of beer here – competitive pricing ensures that all Bamberg breweries have a thriving take out trade.

The bars or guestrooms are entered from the courtyard, the principal of these is likely to be called the Gaststübe or Gastzimmer with perhaps a Nebenzimmer (adjoining room), used as an overflow room, when the main room is full. There may also be a function room (Saal) where wedding and other celebrations can be held.

Inside, the essential "gemütlichkeit" or cosy atmosphere is engendered by the characteristic leaded windows and lace curtains, which diffuse daylight. Walls are usually panelled in wood, below a low timber-beamed ceiling, turned by tobacco smoke and age to shades of dark brown. There are some exceptions – some Gäststatte are more basic and austere with a high ceiling and may be rather too brightly lit. Modernisation in the 1960s and 1970s ruined the interiors of some old pubs, but today a lot more care is likely to be taken to restore them sympathetically. However modernisation is usually done in traditional style and rarely offends although the use of pine cladding in some pubs jars.

Scrubbed tables and solid wooden chairs that scrape the uncarpeted floor are the basic furnishings. The traditional tiled stove, usually resplendent in a vivid shade of green, is a typical but usually redundant feature as nowadays, modern central heating systems are used. Rustic decorations adorn the walls – antlers and other hunting trophies, stuffed animals and birds, dried flowers, farm implements, plates, religious icons, old photographs, engravings, diplomas and other brewing memorabilia. Elaborate ornamental lamps hang over each table.

The bar area is the focus of activity as waiting staff rush to and fro to relay orders and collect drinks. Dark, glass-fronted cupboards house the glasses. The beer fonts are mounted on a copper-topped or stainless steel servery but the actual barrels, if gravity dispense is employed, may be deployed here. Old ceramic mugs are everywhere, often these are examples of real craftsmanship with elaborate tin lids and decoration.

Tables tend to be large and drinkers are expected to move up and allow newcomers to share the table. There's none of the hogging of space and seating that you encounter in Britain, and leaving coats and bags on seats is also frowned upon. Use the pegs provided! In many pubs it is possible to make an advance reservation of a table for a group. This is a different arrangement to the Stammtisch, which is a table reserved for the "regulars", often a weekly meeting of a group of friends or business colleagues. It's usually denoted by an ornamental sign on or above the table in question. Visitors should avoid sitting at a Stammtisch unless specifically invited to do so.

No one who has drunk in Franconian pubs will have failed to notice the strange ritual of knocking on tables. This is simply a local way of greeting or saying goodbye to all those at the table.

The Rauchsverbot

A downside to Franconian pubs was always their smokiness, Germans as a whole being heavy smokers. The *Rauchverbot* (smoking ban) introduced a few years ago restricts smoking to a separate room, if available, or to small pubs (under 75 sq metres floor space) which could elect to be smoking pubs, providing children were not admitted and food (apart from snacks) was not served. Most Bamberg pubs adopted a policy of no smoking in any indoor areas. A vote which might result in a full ban is due to take place in June/July 2010. Gardens and other outside drinking areas are not affected.

Opening and closing hours of pubs

The reality of the situation in Franconia is far removed from the all day opening stereotype of German pubs. Here, traditional pubs tend to open early and close by 23:00, with locals calling in for a beer as early as 08:30. Most pubs have a fixed closing time and will stop serving at this time. Unlike the noisy, uncivilised and confrontational scenes you experience in British pubs, closing time happens quietly here. Waiting staff employ the simple expedient of ignoring further calls for refreshment. Young people's pubs and music bars on the other hand do not open until early evening and stay open well into the early hours. Some pubs in small towns and rural areas may have quite restricted opening times e.g. the brewpubs of Forchheim have extremely complicated opening hours with no apparent logic behind them. One brew-pub in Staffelstein used to open "wenn der Wirt will" – when the owner felt like it! With a largely local clientele the possibility of disappointing casual visitors is not a strong consideration! You cannot always rely on published opening times being correct, and indeed some pubs may publish different opening times in different publications!

Rest days and holidays

Most German pubs have a Ruhetag or rest day, which varies from pub to pub. In smaller towns it is often arranged so that different pubs take their Ruhetag on different days. Some do not close for a whole day but may open late or close early one day a week. As might be expected the Ruhetag normally falls on those days of the week that one would expect to be less busy – Monday to Thursday. However it is not unknown for pubs to close on what might be considered the potentially busiest days – Friday, Saturday or Sunday. The Keesmann brewpub in Bamberg, for example, is closed on Saturday evening and all day Sunday. The Ruhetag may not be clearly advertised outside the pub, except when it is actually in operation and at any time pubs may be inexplicably closed! In fine weather some rural pubs may close with activity transferred to their Keller – a notice stating "Kellerbetrieb" will hopefully indicate if this is the case. The Keller may be some distance away.

Some pubs also close for an annual holiday – this is often taken at the end of the summer tourist season or at the New Year; some may shut for religious holidays. Public holidays in Franconia are listed on page 77.

Service

Table service is the norm in German pubs, with the bill being presented on departure. Even if you are drinking with a group, individual bills are presented, unless you ask to pay "alles zusammen". You can prop up the bar in some pubs – not in the traditional Gaststätte – and pay as you order. Gardens and Kellers are often self-service (selbsbedienung), with a deposit (Pfand) on the mug. It has to be said that service in some Bamberg pubs does not meet modern expectations of customer care and can be slow, abrupt and off-hand, with little allowance made for people whose German isn't up to scratch!

Waiting staff – known as Kellner (male) or Kellnerin (female) work very hard and often appear harassed. Bamberg people tend to be unforgiving of slow service or mistakes by waiting staff!

If your glass is empty, you may be offered a fresh beer without having to summon the waiter or waitress. A beermat placed on your glass indicates that you do not want any more. If drinking from a ceramic mug you should turn the empty mug on its side to indicate that you require another beer.

Other drinking places

Cafés in the Bamberg area, as in the rest of Germany are very different in atmosphere to pubs, although they sell alcoholic drinks. Some cafés are attached to a bakery and are known as Konditorei – these are where you can indulge in the German ritual of coffee and cakes, which is not to be missed! Most however are general street cafés, with ice creams and all. Either way, they are likely to open in the daytime only and the alcoholic drinks will usually include only bottled beer. They may also provide light snacks and lunches.

Bars abound in Bamberg and other major towns and cities and all have their particular raison d'être. Many are small with basic facilities and limited food, and may only sell Pils-type beers. There are many that are music-orientated and attract an exclusively young clientele. Some of these can be quite noisy and rough.

There are hotels to suit all tastes and pockets, from the upmarket establishments with restaurant to the "hotel garni" which does bed and breakfast only and has no bar or restaurant.

It is difficult to draw a distinction between the various Gaststätte, small hotels, and restaurants, and answer the question categorically – can I just have a drink here, or am I expected to order a meal? Most will open all day for food and drink but some positively encourage eating and you might have difficulty in getting a seat let alone just a drink at busy times. Most of the traditional pubs keep a good balance between eating and drinking but the trend is for the old-style Gaststätte to be converted into restaurants with Italian, Spanish, Greek or Chinese food. A few pubs are going over to what is seen as "modern" bistro type food, featuring pasta, pizza, Tex-Mex, vegetarian, or Tapas dishes, or a combination of these. This sort of modernisation invariably means the introduction of a wider range of drinks than is normally found in traditional local pubs – in particular cocktails and bottled "national" beers such as Bitburger and the ubiquitous Desperados. It has also meant the disappearance of pub names that had been in place for centuries.

The tie

Breweries in Bamberg and Franconia rarely own any pubs apart from their own brewery tap and Keller. Pubs not owned by breweries enter into agreements for supply of drinks, which may tie them to a particular brewery's beers for long periods – 5 or 10 years or even more. The owner of the building often enters into this agreement rather than the tenant who is running the pub or restaurant. Therefore, pubs that are free to sell a range of beers from different breweries are unusual in Franconia.

Bamberg's pubs

It would be impossible to review all the hundreds of places, ranging from basic bars to upmarket restaurants, in which one can eat and drink in Bamberg. The following represent my personal selection of Bamberg pubs and hopefully will lead readers to the best in the tradition and enable them to sample a cross section of local beers. Wherever possible, details have been checked with the pubs concerned or with other published sources. Draught beers available are listed; in addition all pubs will have a selection of bottled beer.

Details of Bamberg's breweries and their beers are on pages 15–22 and a list of their beers is in appendix 4 on pages 88–89.

Alt-Ringlein

Dominikanerstraße 9, 96049 Bamberg
T 9532-0
www.alt-ringlein.com

This hotel occupies a prominent site right in the centre of Bamberg opposite Schlenkerla. Said to date from 1545, the picturesque complex of old buildings once housed a brewery, which closed in 1957. Extensive redevelopment took place in the 1980s when today's hotel (20 bedrooms) came into existence. There are several traditional-style rooms and a pleasant outside drinking areas which seats 200.

BEERS: **Mahrs Ungespundetes**, both **Schlenkerla** and **Spezial Rauchbiers**, and "**Ringlas-Helles**", the house beer, which on one visit was served in what appeared to be an original glass from the old brewery!
Open 09:00–01:00

Ambräusianum

Dominikanerstraße 10, 96049 Bamberg
T 5090262
www.ambraeusianum.de
A spacious brew-pub with several different drinking areas arranged around the brewery.

BEERS: **Ambräusianum Hell, Dunkel, Bernsteinweizen, Schlenkerla Rauchbier**.
Open 11:00–23:00 Tuesday to Saturday, 11:00–21:00 Sundays, closed Mondays.

Bamberger Weißbierhaus

Obere Königstraße 38, 96052 Bamberg
T 25503   FAX 25503
www.bamberg-weissbierhaus.de

This was the Brehm brewery tap until it was bought by the Maisel brothers in 1894, after which it became the Maisel-Bräu-Stübl and was designated as the brewery tap of the Maisel brewery, being rather more convenient for the City centre than the Maisel-Keller at the brewery. Since a makeover in 1996 it has been known as the "Bamberger Weißbierhaus". This is a traditional style Bamberg pub, with a quaint old courtyard for fine weather drinking at the rear and a skittle alley. Overnight accommodation is available. The current draught beer selection includes **Mahrs "U"**, **Weismain Pils** and **Maisel Weisse** and **Landbier Dunkel** from Bayreuth. The food includes Franconian and international specialities, with themed evenings.
Open 11:00 to 14:00 and 16:30 to 23:00, Wednesday to Saturday, 16:30 to 23:00 Mondays & Tuesdays, 10:00 to 14:00 Sundays.

Buger Hof

Am Regnitzufer 1, 96049 Bamberg
T 56054
www.buger-hof.de

Brits are naturally vastly amused by the name of this pub! It's a pleasant old place with a large modern extension, run by the same family for generations, in the village of Bug, about three kilometres from Bamberg city centre. You can reach it on bus 918 or by simply following the attractive riverside walk south from Bamberg city centre. Beers from the Schlossbrauerei Reckendorf can be drunk in the pub and on the outside terrace. The overnight accommodation is reasonably priced.
Open: daily except Mondays. It also shuts for a holiday in September.

Café Abseits

Pödeldorferstraße 39, 96052 Bamberg
T 303422
www.abseits.de

Bamberg's leading beer speciality pub, a modernised café-bar with a split-level interior,

noteworthy for promoting a range of local and regional beers with monthly guests; there are usually four draught beers: **Keesmann Pils**, **Huppendorfer Vollbier** and **Weissbier**, **Mönchsambacher Lager** plus a guest, and over 30 bottled beers. Bock beers are featured from October to May. A new feature (2010) is a small range of Belgian beers.

The food encompasses pasta and Tex-Mex as well as more traditional local fare, and all-day breakfasts are a special feature. Abseits has a good website with useful links – it also caters for English speakers, particularly the local American market.

Open 09:00 to midnight every day, beer garden open in summer months until 23:30.

is located in the rather dull area of Bamberg to the east of the station, near the Police headquarters. As there is no back entrance to the station, if on foot you have to approach the pub either from the north going under the railway at Zollnerstraße, or from the south by crossing the Eisenbahnbrücke. Bus 902 is the best way of getting there; bus circular route 911 is useful but it will take you all round east Bamberg before arriving at Katharinenstraße which is a block away from Abseits. The night bus 935 follows a similar route and will also return you to the centre – last bus 00:18 (one hour later on Fridays and Saturdays).

Once a student bar, Abseits does not claim to be a traditional Bamberg pub (the name means literally "the other place"), but it appeals to both locals and visitors. There is a most welcome emphasis on quality and customer satisfaction. Abseits is particularly

Englischer Garten "Zum Bockser"
Schweinfurterstraße 1, 96049 Bamberg
T 61470

The garden is a raised terrace at the back of the pub, a very pleasant place for an evening drink, but there's nothing English about it! There is also a nice traditional room inside the pub, which has a long history but only acquired its present name in 1861. The beer used to come from Maisel, but it is not known which brewery nows supplies the pub. Bus 916.

Open 11:30–14:00 and 16:00–23:00, closed Tuesdays (Unless a public holiday, in which case the pub closes Wednesday instead.

Eulenspiegel
Obere Brücke 10, 96047 Bamberg
T 203052

Named after the jester in the mediaeval German legend – there is an archive dedicated to him at Bamberg University. Situated on the route taking tourists over the upper bridge into the city, there is outside seating café-style and a long narrow bar which opens out at the end. St.Georgen Pils, Landbier and Kellerbier, plus Schlenkerla Rauchbier are on draught. Relatively pricey but in contrast to other nearby bars, a peaceful place for a late night beer – it opens till 03:00!

Fässla

Obere Königstraße19/21, 96052 Bamberg
T 26516   FAX 201989
www.faessla.de

This is an excellent family-run brewery guest-
house. Over the last 20 years substantial
refurbishment has taken place, but has not
spoilt the traditional atmosphere of this
archetypal Bamberg pub. The original two bars
are unchanged, and a new room has been
added to the left as you enter the pub. Beyond
the corridor with its bench seats, where the
locals gather as soon as the pub opens, there
is a little courtyard for outside drinking in
summer; this is self service and drinks have
to be ordered and paid for at the *Schenke*.
This is also a smoking area. With modernised
accommodation offering good value, Fässla
is very welcoming and a good base for a
Bamberg holiday – but book well in advance.
Open 09:00 to 23:00, it closes at 13:00 on Sundays,
on which day no food is served.

Fässla-Keller

Moosstraße 32, 96050 Bamberg
T 29516

This pub and garden was the brewery tap of
Maisel, and was acquired by Fässla after the
closure of Maisel in 2008. Whilst the pub only
dates back to 1934 and is situated quite a
way out of town (bus 911 & 921), it's worth a
visit. In particular, the garden is very pleasant
on a summer's evening. There is good value
food and a children's play area.
Open 11:00 to 23:00.

Fässla beers

Greifenklau

Laurenziplatz 20, 96049 Bamberg
T 53219
www.greifenklau.de

A stiff climb up from the Altstadt (bus 908, 912
or 918 will help) to the summit of the Kaulberg,
Greifenklau is situated in an enclave of 17th
century houses off the old road to Würzburg.
This is a lovely old tavern, low ceilinged and
dimly lit. The equally attractive, shady beer
garden behind the pub is very popular and has
500 seats and an excellent view across a wooded
valley to the picturesque old Altenburg castle.
Open 10:30 to 23:00, On Sundays it opens 10:00 and closes
14:00, but not before a hearty roast lunch has been served.
The pub is also closed Mondays and during Sandkerwa.

Griesgarten

Untere Sandstraße 19, 96049 Bamberg
T 56754

There is a very good traditional atmosphere
in this pub in the old city, which serves **Krug
Bauernbier** and **Pils**. This brewery closed many
years ago and the beer, once contract brewed
by the Werner brewery at Poppenhausen, now
apparently comes from Hofbräu in Würzburg.
There is also good traditional food. The pleasant garden at the rear is very popular; note the
large green wooden structure which is a
shooting gallery.
Opens 11:00 to midnight, closed Wednesdays except May to
September when it opens at 17:00 to midnight.

Kachelhofen

Obere Sandstraße 1, 96049 Bamberg
T 57172
www.zumkachelofen.de

Taking its name from the tiled stove that is a common source of heating in traditional pubs, this pleasant Bierstübe is notable for its charming interior which has plenty of cosy nooks as well as the eponymous stove. Also notable is its hearty Franconian cuisine. You won't starve here, particularly if you opt for the sausage platter, but it's more for meat-eaters than vegetarians! **St.Georgen Pils** and **Kellerbier** from Buttenheim, and **Schlenkerla Rauchbier**, are on draught. In fine weather, benches outside enable you to sit and watch the world go by in the heart of the old city.
Open daily 10:00 to 01:00, food served to 23:00.

Kaiserdom-Brauereigasthof & Hotel

Gaustadter Hauptstraße 26, 96049 Bamberg-Gaustadt
T 965140   FAX 9651444
www.hotel-kaiserdom.de

This, the former Burgerbräu brewery, is now the Kaiserdom brewery tap, upmarket and modernised in the Kaiserdom style, with an emphasis on food. Drinkers can sit at the bar, and enjoy a selection of draught beers. In summer there is a decent sized, shady garden. Buses 906 and 916 will take you to Gaustadt.
Open 07:00 to 13:30, 17:30 to 23:00 Tuesday to Saturday, Sundays from 11:30. Closed Mondays.

Keesmann

Wunderburg 5, 96050 Bamberg
T 9819810
www.keesmann-braeu.de (under development)

A very traditional brewpub in the suburb of Wunderburg, reached by bus 905 from Bamberg bus station. The opening hours themselves define the clientele. There is a dedicated local following and all the expected traditional atmosphere. The bar is lighter and airier than is usual in Bamberg taverns, dating back to a refurbishment in the 1980s, but the clientele

is typical of Bamberg – the enthusiastically played card and domino games can be extremely noisy! Brotzeit is devoured with relish. The entrance hall leads through to a beer garden in the courtyard behind the pub, with the brewery enclosing it on two sides.
Open 09:00 to 23:00, but closed Saturdays from 15:00 and all day Sundays.

Klosterbräu

Ob. Mühlbrücke 1–3, 96049 Bamberg
T 52265
www.klosterbraeu.de

Following quaint old lanes from the Altstadt, you come to this picturesque old brewery. Incredibly, there was no brewery tap prior to June 1988 and the current Gaststätte has been created in stages since then. The small panelled room known as the Braunbier-Stübla, on the left as you enter the brewery, was the first to be opened. There is now a restaurant, and function rooms in the old tithe house and vaults. In fine weather, there is further seating in the brewery courtyard, and outside on the street. The latest addition (2009) is a very attractive beer garden overlooking the river. Draught beers usually include **Pils**, **Braunbier** and **Schwärzla**.
Open 10:30 (10:00 Saturdays and holidays) to 23:00 (22:00 Sundays).

Mahr's Bräu

Wunderburg 10, 96050 Bamberg
T 9151719
www.mahrs-braeu.de

This superb brewery tap, beloved of British visitors, is not to be missed. It's situated next to the church in the suburb of Wunderburg, and can be reached by bus 905. There are two traditional rooms, one of which is particularly atmospheric with its low ceilings, tiled stove and beers served direct from wooden barrels. "Zum Brenner" is another room at the back of the pub and is open in the evening. The draught beers usually include **Helles** and the **ungespundetes Lagerbier**, which is usually tapped at 17:00. The corridor of the pub is famous for its gathering of locals from all walks of life for the "Stehgammler", a stand-up drinking tradition of locals, described as a "Stammtisch ohne Tisch". The courtyard at the front serves as a beer garden in fine weather and is shaded by ancient chestnut trees. There is a good range of brewery merchandise, displayed in a shop front between the brewery and the church, and these can be purchased from the brewery office during brewery opening hours. Horse-drawn coach rides are available Easter to October and will take you from the old city to the brewery and back for a small fee which includes a beer token.

Open 09:00 to 23:00.

Michaelsberg Café & Restaurant

Michaelsberg 10g, 96049 Bamberg
T 2085777

The buildings of the great monastery of the Michaelsberg date back to the mid-eighteenth century when it was rebuilt to plans by Balthasar Neumann. In the course of secularisation in 1804 the Benedictine monastery was dissolved and passed over to the Citizens' Hospital Foundation [*Bürgerspitalstiftung*]. Today this still cares for Bamberg's elderly and infirm. In 2003 the former brewery tap, the Gaststätte Michaelsberg Benediktinerbräu, was converted to an Italian restaurant and this fine traditional pub, with its pleasant little beergarden was lost. However, around the back of the church is this not very pubby establishment (a nice panelled room, but white tablecloths!) which is quite old-fashioned and not the place to go if you're in a hurry. It has a reasonable selection of beers, which seems to change from time to time, including a **dark bock** from Vierzehnheiligen which I have not encountered anywhere else. Outside, there are superb views over the city from the terrace. The food includes a salad buffet.

Open 10:00 to 22:30, closed Tuesdays except in summer.

Pelikan

Untere Sandstraße 45, 96049 Bamberg
T 603410
www.pelikan.de (under development)

A lively pub with a variety of beers, which include the highly recommended **Huppendorfer Vollbier** and the new **Stegaurach** beer on draught. Food with a Thai theme is served until Midnight.

Open 17:00–01:00, 17:00–02:00 Friday & Saturday

Schlenkerla

Dominikanerstraße 6, 96049 Bamberg
T 56060 (56050 for table reservations)
www.schlenkerla.de

The historic brewery tap of Heller-Brau Trum is in the heart of the old city. The exceptionally dark and smoky **Aecht Schlenkerla Rauchbier** is served direct from the wooden barrel, with the stronger **Ur-Bock** available from October until Christmas. Two large traditional rooms, one of which (the "Alte Lokal") is the typical Bamberg room, dark and low ceilinged, the other (the "Klause") being more austere with ecclesiastical vaulting – it was once the chapel of a 14th Century Dominican Priory. The central corridor has some seating but is primarily a stand-up drinking area, with self-service from the *Schenke*. It also has a kiosk selling takeouts and souvenirs. Buy your take-outs here rather than at the tourist shops nearby, which are far more expensive. Note how the waiting staff use a system of counters to account for their beer takings.

Schlenkerla is immensely popular and always crowded, but you'll usually manage to

squeeze in. Fortunately, it retains its traditional ambience despite being first port of call on the tourist circuit. The beer garden is now open from Easter to October in good weather. The food is very traditional, a highlight being the Bamberg Onions (see recipe on page 70) and coffee and cola drinks are not sold! Snacks are served from 09:30, hot meals from 12:00 to 22:00.
Open 0930 to 23:30. No Ruhetag or annual holiday.
Closed 25/26 December, 31 December and 1 January.

Spezial

Obere Königstraße 10, 96052 Bamberg
T 24304   FAX 26330
www.brauerei-spezial.de

This brewpub occupies a wonderful old building with half timbering and window boxes full of geraniums. Busy and lively, it's one of the classic pubs of Bamberg with a genuine, traditional atmosphere. **Spezial Rauchbier** is on draught along with the new **Ungespundetes Lagerbier**, which is not a smoke beer. There is a small beer garden in the courtyard, which has only been opened in fairly recent times. The accommodation is good value although there are only seven rooms.
Open 09:00 to 22:00, closes 14:00 on Saturdays.
Closed over Christmas and the New Year.

Sternla

Langestraße 46, 96047 Bamberg
T 28750
www.sternla.de

Sternla ("the little star") is Bamberg's oldest pub, with a list of licensees going back to 1385. Rudolf Maisel acquired it in 1911 and it sold Maisel beer until the demise of that brewery in 2008. This is a traditional pub (the menu is in German and local dialect) with a courtyard for fine weather drinking and good-value food. **Spezial Rauchbier, Mahrs U, Keesmann Pils** and **Sternla**, and **Tucher Hefeweisse**, are on draught.
Open every day 1000 to 2300.

Stöhrenkeller

Obere Stephansberg 11, 96049 Bamberg
T 3020778
www.stoehrenkeller.de

This is a great late-night venue. Many years ago this was the Keller for one of Bamberg's many breweries but in more recent times it was one of Bamberg's best-known pubs with a great character of a landlord. Then it had a spell as an up-market restaurant, and it is from this period that some of the internal decoration dates! It is now owned by the Keesmann family and **Keesmann Pils** in on draught as well as a changing beer from country breweries near Bamberg. There is also a selection of bottled beers, and light snacks are served.
Open from 20:00 every evening until late, except Sunday.

Weinstube Pizzini

Obere Sandstraße 17, 96049 Bamberg
T 56389

A pub of great character, the lady licensee being something of a legend. A good atmosphere is enhanced by wood panelling, tiled stove and high backed settles for intimate drinking. The music also draws approval. A good range of draught beers, which have changed from time to time.
BEERS: **Keesmann Pils** and **Schlenkerla Rauchbier**. Snack menu.
Open from 2000 until late, closed Sundays.

Try also –
pubs recommended by beer enthusiasts who have visited Bamberg

Fässla Stub'n

Kleberstraße 9, 96047 Bamberg

T 120 9961

Semi-basement bar with music, catering for a student clientele. You can enjoy draught **Fässla Zwergla**, which is not available in the Fässla tap. This is a smoking bar.

Open from 17:00.

Hofbräu

Karolinenstraße 7, 96049 Bamberg

T 53321

www.hofbraeu-bamberg.de

An ancient stone-built building with a modernised interior. Formerly a fount of the eponymous brewery, this food-orientated establishment offers four draught beers and the opportunity to drink outside in fine weather.

Open 10:00–01:00, 10:00–02:00 (Sats)

Schmitt's Café

Michaelsberg 29a (corner of Storchgasse)

T 5009903

Löwenbrau Buttenheim Kellerbier on draught.

Open 10:00–22:00 (Mon–Fri), 11:00–22:00 (Sats & Suns)

Stilbruch

Obere Sandstraße 18, 96049 Bamberg

T 5190002

www.stilbruch-bamberg.de

This pub has the slogan "die Kneipe mit Frosch" – the pub with frog! It occupies the former premises of the Grüner Wald brewery which ceased brewing in 1915. The regular draught beers here are **Mahrs U** and **Keesmann Herren Pils**, but on Sunday at 17:00 the tapping of a barrel of **Ottobier** from the Otto Huebner brewery in Steinfeld is eagerly awaited.

Open 19:00–24:00 Mon–Thursday, 19:00–01:00 Fri & Sat, 11:00–24:00 Sundays

Tambosi

Promenadestraße 11, 96047 Bamberg

T 23047

An old-fashioned and traditional town-centre Gaststätte by the bus station. **Helles**, **Pils** and **Kellerbier** came from the now defunct Schmitt-Bräu of Schesslitz; it is unclear who brews the beers now. Tambosi is a more of a "lunchtime" pub, catering for working people and the older generation with a menu that offers high quality, home-cooked traditional food and is very good value. There is now a beer garden.

Open 09:00 to 21:00, closed Sundays.

Tapas-Bar

Untere Kaulberg 36

T 5190518

www.tapas-bamberg.de

This is the former Röckelein brewery, which ceased brewing in 1968, although the brewing operation had moved some years previously to the Keller up the hill at Laurenzistrasse. It has had a number of name changes over the years but still has one original feature – a wonderful view of the cathedral from its terrace. The beer selection includes **Mönchsambacher Lager** which is well worth seeking out.

Open 17:00, 12:00 at weekends and public holidays.

Torchuster

Obere Karolinenstraße 10

T 55508

The "cobbler at the gate" occupies what is effectively a gatehouse by the old city walls. Bus 10 from the city centre stops outside. It's a tiny pub which changed hands a few years ago and now specialises in serving a variety of Bamberg beers, two of which – **Mahrs U** and **Keesmann Herren Pils** – are on draught.

Opens at 18:00 daily.

Marc Buchner's cartoons, penned in *Dialekt*, reflect his very special insight into Bamberg life and the city's beer culture. His cartoons appear in the local Fränkische Nacht magazine.
His amusing views on Bamberg life are brought to life by the character "farmer Böhnlein" who appears in many of the cartoons and whose cantankerous nature usually involves a surfeit of beer!

Farmer Böhnlein takes exception to a tourist using a mobile phone in a beer garden (Keller), although British beer drinkers would also take exception to the fact that he is clearly a "beer bore"! This cartoon was actually written in English!

This ferocious Bamberg waitress appears in many of Marc's cartoons. The character is said to be based on a waitress who once worked at one of Bamberg's brew-pubs! The customer has made the error of asking for "a beer, please" rather than the customary local request "a Seidla". A tourist will usually be forgiven.

"A beer, please!"   *"What?"*   *"a Seidla!" "he's learning already!!"*

"So, a smoke beer!" *"Ah, the local speciality!"...*   *"Would you like another?!"*

"There's your beer!"
"You ought to be friendlier!"   *"Friendly?!*
I'm going to smack you one!!!"   *"He's lucky,*
I'm in a good mood today!"

Kellers and gardens:
a unique outside drinking tradition

In Franconia the term Bierkeller or Sommerkeller causes confusion to foreign or North German visitors. They are surprised to find that Kellers are not smoky dives situated in a cellar under a pub, but beer gardens that open on the hills outside towns in the summer months. The name originates in the days before refrigeration when beer was brewed in the winter months and stored or lagered in cool cellar caves in the hills for summer consumption. They are now one of the most delightful features of beer drinking in Franconia, and thankfully remain simple establishments with basic benches and tables, and rarely provide anything sophisticated in the way of food.

There are dozens of Kellers in the Franconian countryside owned by pubs that once used them to lager their own brew. Most pubs that still brew have their own Keller although these days the beer is usually lagered in a refrigerated room at the brewery.

Most of Bamberg's breweries had their own Keller mainly on the Stephansberg but in some cases on the Jakobsberg or Kaulberg. After brewing, the beer would be taken by the traditional beer wagon to the Keller for lagering.

The origins of the Franconian beer Kellers go back to the early days of beer, to the time when bottom fermenting beer was first recognised in the Nabburger chronicles of 1474. This type of beer could be stored for 9–10 months but the problem was storing it in cool conditions so that it would survive over the summer months. This was achieved in country areas by storing the beers in tunnels in hillsides where temperatures would remain stable. Where possible, such tunnels were established on north-facing slopes, and trees, usually chestnuts, were planted to give additional shade. Eventually these Kellers attracted custom and beer was served direct from the stores. With provision of table and benches they developed naturally into a brewery tap for the summer months. Thus began a great regional tradition.

In Upper Franconia this had a significant effect, as wine had always been the traditional summer drink. In 1831 Bamberg had 40 premises serving wine in addition to 62 breweries. The balance was soon to swing in favour of beer. From 1830 onwards a Keller boom took place. People would end their country walks at a Keller or find the quickest route to one. In 1835 the Stegauracher publicans actually laid on transport to attract custom. Numerous advertisements appeared in the press to encourage a Keller visit and the Bamberger Tagesblatt newspaper set up a Keller enquiry office in 1838.

Increasing competition induced new ideas for attracting customers. Bowling, shooting stalls (the Forchheim Annafest originated this way) and music pavilions, for example at Wilde Rose in Bamberg, were amongst the attractions.

Every boom runs its course. In 1840 there were 63 summer Kellers in the Bamberg area but by the turn of the century there were only 35. The First World War contributed to a further decline, and at the end of that conflict only the Mahrs and Spezial Kellers remained open out of 21 that had originally been situated on the Stephansberg. By 1934 there were only 11 left in Bamberg. Even today one can see the sites of disused Kellers.

Today, the situation is much improved. The triangle enclosed by Bamberg, Bayreuth and Erlangen is a summer Keller region without rival and the popularity of the region's Kellers has led to a recent revival, including the rehabilitation of disused sites. A recent idea by publicans to increase the attraction of Kellers is to provide children's play areas.

(from Kellerführer 1 by Peter Sem).

Beer gardens and Kellers only open in fine weather, usually during the period May to September but in the event of exceptional weather may open at other times of year – the Bamberg Kellers have been known to open in February. "Fine weather" means effectively a prospect of continuing fine weather, as most Kellers have no shelter to retire to in the event of sudden rain. Some Kellers do have a pub with indoor seating on the site, which may be open all year round, irrespective of weather conditions, or only when the outside area is open. Kellers are usually only open late afternoons and sometimes only at weekends. Simple food is usually available but you can bring your own food and enjoy a picnic. Going "auf den Keller" is a popular outing for Franconian families and friends.

Recommended Kellers and gardens in Bamberg

The following are some of Bamberg's most original and attractive beergardens and Kellers. Many pubs have a beer garden in the British sense – a garden next to the pub for al fresco drinking. Other pubs use their courtyard – around here any opportunity to drink outside in fine weather is seized upon.

Bootshaus

Mühlworth 18a, **T** 24485
Near the Hainbad open-air swimming pool, this is part of a functioning boat house used by rowers on the river Regnitz. Bootshaus has a marvellous riverside setting and views. Opens 11:00 to 01:00 in fine weather, in the author's experience it has to be very fine weather. The draught beer selection includes **Kraus** from Hirschaid.

Mahrs-Keller

Obere Stephansberg 36, **T** 53486
www.mahrsbraeu-keller.de
Restored and brought back into use in the 1980s, this attractive old timbered building is really a pub/restaurant with a small but pleasant, tree-shaded garden rather than a traditional Keller. It's well known for food, particularly its "Bierkulinarium" or beer cuisine. To wash it down, there's **Mahrs Pils**, "**Gig**" and **Weisse** on draught. The pub is open from 17:00 every day except Mondays, and is also open for lunch on Sundays and holidays.

Spezial-Keller

Sternwartstraße, **T** 54887
At the popular "Spezi-Keller", **Rauchbier** from the wooden barrel complements a superb view of the city in this 800-seat garden. It's a treat to watch the sun set behind the spires. The entrance is just off the Stephansberg by the Schlenkerla brewery – just follow Sternwartstrasse round. There is also a pub on the site, which is very much in the style of Spezial's city pub, and this is open all year round. The garden is only open in fine weather, when the

path which provides a short cut to the garden will be open. Open 15:00 daily (10:00 Sundays and holidays), closed Mondays. Some seats in the garden are designated "self-service" and you can go up to the serving area for drinks and snacks.

Villa Remeis
St.Getreustraße 13
A cosy café located in an early nineteenth century villa, once the home of Dr. Karl Remeis, the astronomer. Opens 11:00–18:00, closed Mondays. The outside seating enjoys superb views of Bamberg, which is the reason for coming here – the beers are from Mahrs, but bottled only – no draught. Bus 910 to the Villa Remeis stop.

Wilde Rose Bräu Keller
Ob. Stephansberg 49, **T** 57691
A large attractive garden with an old music pavilion, which is still used for live music concerts from time to time. However, there are no views.This garden is self-service with a deposit (Pfand) on mugs. The house beer – **draught Kellerbier** and **Weissbier** is specially

brewed for this Keller, the brewery is unknown. Wilde Rose's parent hotel in the Kesslerstraße was once a brewery. Buses 908 and 928 to Hohes Kreuz avoid the need for a long walk uphill from the city – although natives will claim this is part of the "Keller experience"! Wilde Rose is open from 16:00 to 23:00, (15:00 Sats and Suns).

Other Kellers and gardens can be found at Greifenklau, Griesgarten, Mahrs-Bräu, the Fässla-Keller, and the Michaelsberg. See under "Bamberg pubs".

The website www.bierkeller.de has a huge amount of information about the local Keller culture and also provides an opportunity for enthusiasts to vote for their Keller of the year! Recent winners in the contest, run by Radio Bamberg and the *Fränkischer Tag* newspaper, have been

2009 – Die Radspitzeinkehr, Marktrodach
2008 – Erlauer Biergarten Kiessling, Erlau
2007 – Brauerei Kundmüller, Weiher

Around Bamberg – breweries in the Landkreis Bamberg

This administrative area contains over 70 breweries most of which can be reached fairly easily from Bamberg. Here's a selection listed by location.

The walking tours are just suggestions – there is no room to include further detail about the route to take, but enough facts are given so that with a map and this and other published guide books, and a check on transport times, you should be able to have an enjoyable walk and some good beer.

Baunach

Baunach is a village on the edge of the Hassberge Nature Park, about 10 kilometres from Bamberg (rail service). The very small Brauerei Sippel brews a dark **Vollbier**, available only in this family run pub and beergarden. There is overnight accommodation and a Wednesday Ruhetag is observed.

Brauerei Sippel, Burgstraße 20, 96148 Baunach. **T** 09544 2488

Bischberg

About five kilometres from Bamberg city centre and easily reached by city bus no.906. The Zur Sonne brewpub on the main street is of very ancient origin – 1587 to be precise, and has been run by the Schuhmann family for 150 years. Good food and local atmosphere. Sonne brews a pleasant pale **Vollbier** ("Urtyp Hell"), which is also available in their nearby beergarden, Schuhmann's Keller. To find this, turn off the main street at the Apotheke into Rothofweg. Zur Sonne is closed on Tuesdays. There is a Kirchweih in Bischberg around the first Sunday in September

Hausbrauerei zur Sonne, Regnitzstraße 2, 96120 Bischberg. **T** 0951 62571 www.sonnenbier.de

Buttenheim

On the Bamberg-Nürnberg railway line, this small town is in fact a few kilometres from the railway station of the same name and has two breweries. Its only other claim to fame is as the birthplace of Levi Strauss, the jeans man, to whom a museum in the town is dedicated. St.Georgen Bräu's beers are widely available in this part of Franconia. The brewery Bräustübla has **Pils** and the outstanding **Kellerbier** on draught. Thursday is Ruhetag. Next door is the much smaller Löwenbräu with a nice basic taproom and restaurant serving a Kellerbier in tin-lidded mugs. Monday is Ruhetag. Both pubs have accommodation. Don't miss the Kellers: turn right out of the breweries and right again, cross the road leading to the motorway and you will soon find the Löwenbräu Keller on the right. This is open daily from 11:00 to 23:00 but is closed September to April on Tuesday and Wednesday. The St.Georgen Keller is further on down a road to the left, and is open daily from 15:00 (14:00 Sundays and holidays).

Löwenbräu, Marktstraße 8, 96155 Buttenheim, **T** 09545 332 www.loewenbraeu-buttenheim.de

St. Georgen Bräu, Marktstraße 12, 96155 Buttenheim, **T** 09545 4460, Bräustübla **T** 09545 950160, www.kellerbier.de

Dörfleins & Hallstadt

Dörfleins is a small village to the north west of Bamberg, beyond Hallstadt, which itself is virtually a suburb of Bamberg. The 904 bus gets you there in about 20 minutes, but note that although not all services on this route go as far as Dörfleins, you can easily walk there from Hallstadt. The village pub is the Schwarzer Adler which houses the Eichhorn brewery. Open 09:00 to 23:00 (1900 Thursdays, 2000 Saturdays, closed Monday. The late John White described it as "a simple, traditional, multi-roomed gem".
Brauerei Schwarzer Adler, Dörfleinserstraße 43, 96103 Dörfleins. **T** 0951 75660, www.brauerei-eichhorn.de

Hallstadt has the Goldenen Löwen pub, once home to the Lowenbräu Diller brewery, which closed in 1985. This is a wonderful old building with a basic interior, and its beers now come from the Hönig brewery at Tiefenellern, so are well worth seeking out. There are several other pubs in Hallstadt including a pub with Fässla beers.

WALKING TOUR 1
A stroll from Strullendorf

This 17 km walk is described by Helmut Herrmann in his booklet "Biergarten – wanderungen in Franken", and is also featured in great detail on the late John White's website. There is an hourly rail service from Bamberg to Strullendorf. The walk takes in Geisfeld and Roßdorf (see the entries for these villages), and also the highly-recommended Schwanenkeller in Strullendorf itself, which is about one mile from the station and sells Löwenbräu beer from Buttenheim. Strullendorf no longer has a functioning brewery of its own, alas. However, to ensure that you make the most of the Kellers en route, a Sunday excursion is recommended, and a map such as the Kompass 1:50,000 map (no. 171, Fränkische Schweiz).

Drosendorf

A small village which is easily accessible by bus 907 from Bamberg. The Brauerei Göller brews an **ungespundete Lagerbier** and **Urstoff**, a pale amber beer. There is an extensive beergarden, and a further covered drinking area next to the modern pub. You'll get a warm welcome from the English-speaking owner, whose family have run the business since its foundation in 1865. Monday Ruhetag.
Brauerei Göller, Scheßlitzerstraße 7, 96117 Drosendorf. **T** 09505 1745

Geisfeld

The modern pub of the Griess brewery is about seven kilometres from Bamberg and is open 15:00 daily, 10:00 weekends, Wednesday is Ruhetag. The popular Griess-Keller is a short distance away from the village. The Metzner bus service from Bamberg serves Geisfeld but it is also an easy cycle ride along a well sign-posted route. The attractive half-timbered building that stands at the entrance to the former cellar caves is much-photographed. It is now used as a servery where the **Griess Keller-bier** comes direct from the barrel. Open 16:30 daily, 14:00 Sundays, in fine weather only.
Brauerei-Gasthof Griess, Magdalenen-straße 6, 96129 Geisfeld, **T** 09505 1624 www.brauerei-griess.de or www.griess-keller.de

Herrnsdorf

The highly regarded Brauerei Barnikel produces **Lagerbier** and **Rauchbier**, the former on draught and the latter in flip-top bottles. A family business with a farm and schnaps distillery, located in a small village, this pub's history can be traced back to 1366! Wednesday is Ruhetag. About 10 kilometres from Hirschaid on the Bamberg–Nürnberg railway, but served by occasional regional buses from Bamberg. Try also the Brauerei Kraus in Hirschaid itself (closed Tuesdays).

Brauerei Friedrich Barnikel, Dorfstraße 5, 96158 Frensdorf-Herrnsdorf. **T** 09502 293.

Huppendorf

This farming village near Scheßlitz has been home to the Grasser brewery and pub for over 250 years. The **Huppendorfer Vollbier** is a particularly quaffable medium-dark Lagerbier. Closed Tuesdays.

Brauerei Johannes Grasser, 96167 Huppendorf. **T** 09207 270. www.huppendorfer-bier.de

Kemmern

A village located a few kilometres north of Bamberg, served by trains to nearby Breiten-gußbach. Wagner-Bräu is an excellent basic and old-fashioned brewpub, serving **Pils** and in summer an **ungespundetes Lagerbier**. Thursday is Ruhetag. Wagner also has a large beergarden overlooking the valley of the river Main (the Waldfelsenkeller) which is open daily in summer from 1500. Nearby is Leicht's Keller with Reckendorf beer.

Wagner-Brau, Hauptstraße 15, 96164 Kemmern. **T** 09544 6746, www.brauerei-wagner.de.

Memmelsdorf

This village lies a few kilometres east of Bamberg (frequent buses on routes 907, 917 & 927 – journey time 20 minutes), with two brewpubs on the main street, which is very busy with traffic.

Drei Kronen dates back to 1457 and its name is a symbol of the biblical three kings who are the patron saints of travellers. Drei Kronen brews an **"ungespundete" Lagerbier** plus a **Pils** and a unique **"Kellerrauchbier"** called **"Stöffla"**. Accommodation is available in the modernised hotel (**T** 0951 41023). Drei Kronen is closed from 1500 Sundays until 1700 Mondays. The Brauerei Höhn has a very smart and modern Gaststätte offering the sole house beer, **Görchla**. Tuesday Ruhetag. There is also a large beer-garden open in the summer months in Meedens-dorferstraße. Leichtbräu is much more down to earth but unfortunately ceased brewing about 10 years ago. Beer is now supplied from Püls-Brau of Weismain. It is closed on Wednesdays. Accommodation is also available here.

Brauerei-Gasthof Drei Kronen, Hauptstraße 19, 96117 Memmelsdorf. **T** 0951 944330, www.drei-kronen-memmelsdorf.de
Brauerei Höhn, Hauptstraße 11, 96117 Memmelsdorf. **T** 0951 406140 www.gasthof-hoehn.de

Merkendorf

A small village which can be reached by bus service 917 from Bamberg (not Sundays), or by walking from Drosendorf – see walking tour 2 below. Merkendorf is home to two brewpubs, which are both superb examples of the Franconian tradition. Hummel brews a wide range of beers. On my last visit, **Pils**, **Kellerbier** and **Raücherla** were on draught.

The latter is one of the smokiest Rauchbiers I have tried outside Schlenkerla! It observes a Tuesday Ruhetag and opens at 15:00 on Sundays and holidays. There is a separate Keller in Ausstraße. Accommodation is available. Hummel beer can also be found at the Hofcafe in Bamberg's Ausstraße. Round the corner by the church, Wagner has an **ungespundete Lagerbier** which can also be enjoyed in the large garden behind the pub. There is also a vast hall for village celebrations. Monday Ruhetag. **Brauerei Hummel**, Lindenstraße 9, 96117 Merkendorf. **T** 09542 12 47 www.brauerei-hummel.de
Brauerei Wagner, Pointstraße 1, 96117 Merkendorf. **T** 0 95 42 6 20 http://www.wagner-merkendorf.de.

WALKING TOUR 2

Merkendorf

Take the no. 907 bus from Bamberg to the terminus at Drosendorf, where the Göller brewery is just across the road from the bus stop. After a leisurely Seidla, you can walk up the road opposite, which leads to Merkendorf – about three kilometres. After a bend in the road, you pass under the Autobahn, after which a cycle path runs parallel with the road over open fields, Merkendorf being clearly visible in the distance. Arriving in the village, Hummel is on your right. Keep on around to the left by the church and you will find Wagner. Avoid Mondays and Tuesdays and note that Hummel does not open until 15:00 on Sundays and holidays.

Mönchsambach

This village is home to the Zehendner brewpub. The brewery is very much up-to-date but the old pub has an idyllic courtyard and garden. None of the Zehendner beers is filtered. The **Mönchsambacher Lager**, now very popular among Bamberg's beer lovers, is particularly full-bodied with a high hop rate, and there are Bock beers for Christmas and in May. Closed Mondays.
Brauerei Zehendner, 96138 Mönchsambach, **T** 09546 380, www.brauerei-zehendner.de

Reundorf

The Schmausenkeller is a few kilometres from the village of Reundorf, where its parent brewpub, Müller is situated. It is unusual in that the beer is still lagered at the Keller as it would have been centuries ago – most breweries now lager their beer in the brewery. You are likely to find owner and brewer Herr Müller serving at the old Keller entrance, whilst behind him in the caves the beer is lagering in tanks. The **Müller beer** is a rich, spicy blend of hops and malt. The hilltop site has a wonderful view over the surrounding countryside. The Keller site has been extensively developed recently with an attractive new timbered Gaststätte providing food service – this is open whatever the weather. The pub in the village is only open in the winter months, the Keller opens Mid-March to Mid-October from 16:00 (11:00 Sundays), closed Mondays if wet.
Müller-Bräu, Lange Straße 2, 96158 Reundorf. **T** 09502 280 (brewery), **T** 09502 608 (Keller)

Roßdorf am Forst

Eight kilometres to the south-east of Bamberg, Brauerei Sauer is a village-centre pub with an extensive outside drinking area, serving "Urbräu", an unfiltered **Lagerbier**. The pub is closed Mondays. Sauer has an attractive Keller not far from the pub.
Brauerei Sauer, Sutte 5, 96129 Roßdorf am Forst. **T** 09543 1578, www.brauerei-sauer.de

Sauer Keller

Schammelsdorf

A village which lies a few kilometres east of Memmelsdorf – there are a few buses on service bus 927 from Bamberg, but not at weekends. Brauerei Knoblach is a modernised pub that still has a "local" feel. **Lagerbier** is served from the wooden barrel, and the pub has its own schnaps distillery. The food includes the local speciality Zwetschgenbames (thinly sliced beef smoked over plum wood). Closed Mondays.

Brauerei Knoblach, Kremmelsdorfer Straße 1, 96123 Schammelsdorf. **T** 09505 267

Scheßlitz

A ride on regional bus 8224 from Bamberg brings you to this small town with two (until recently three) breweries on the main street. The Barth-Senger brewpub produces a dark Vollbier in its tiny brewery, and serves it from the wooden barrel. Closes from 17:00 on Saturday, and has a Monday Ruhetag. At Drei Kronen, you can drink **"Schäazer Kronabier"** (Schäaz is local dialect for Scheßlitz) in another old-fashioned taproom. This is a pale **Vollbier**, and naturally it's served from a wooden barrel. There is also an unusual **Weizen Bock** in season. Drei Kronen closes 13:00 on Wednesdays. Scheßlitz is on the borders of "Franconian Switzerland" and a possible walking excursion takes you up into the hills, to the ruined castle at Giech and the chapel on the Gügel hill where there is a pub. From here you could return via Köttensdorf (Brauerei Hoh opens mid-afternoon except Wednesday when it is Ruhetag) to Memmelsdorf and the local buses for Bamberg. Or, you could go east to Würgau and Brauerei Hartmann (q.v.)

Brauerei Drei Kronen, Hauptstraße 39, 96110 Scheßlitz, **T** 09542 1564 **www.kronabier.de**
Brauerei Senger, Oberend 11, 96110 Scheßlitz, **T** 09542 1064

Stegaurach region

A scenic area easily reached by bus 912 from Bamberg, the Aurach valley is famous for its carp fisheries. Unfortunately Stegaurach's two brewpubs – the picturesque Windfelder and Krug-Bräu ceased brewing in 1983 and 1990 respectively. You can however still drink Bamberg beer at the pubs, and on the bus route are the brewpubs of Müller at Debring (closed Mondays) and "Zur alten Mühle" at Mühlendorf (closed Tuesdays, accommodation). The Hausbräu Stegaurach brewery, which opened in 2000 and improbably combines brewing with the hire of marquees, has no tap in the village but the beers can be drunk in Bamberg at Pelikan and Catwheezle's Castle.
Hausbrau Stegaurach, Ruhlstraße 6, 96135 Stegaurach, **T** 0951 299709 **www.hausbraeu-stegaurach.de**

Trabelsdorf

The formerly rather low-key Brauerei Beck has been transformed by the arrival of a new brewing team and an enterprising new range of beers: **Pils, Zwickel-Pils, Weiße, Kellerbier, Jahrhundertbier, Lisberger Lager**, a **pale Bock** in season, and a unique triple smoke Bock, **Affumicator** (9.6% ABV), which is already gaining a reputation outside Franconia. The pub is only open from 16:00 Friday and 15:00 on Saturdays and Sundays. There is now a traditional menu. "Zoigl" brewery tours with tasting take place on Tuesday evenings.

The regional bus from Bamberg stops outside, but the service is infrequent.
Brauerei Beck, Steigerwaldstraße 6–8, 96170 Trabelsdorf. **T** 09549-988999 (brewery), **T** 09549 252 (Gaststätte), www.beck-braeu.de

Tiefenellern
Brauerei Hönig produces **Lagerbier**, **Pils**, **Postillion Weisse** and **Postillion Rauchbier**, and a **Bock** in season, and serves them at its pub Zur Post in this remote and rural village, although they are also available at pubs across the region. Closed on Thursdays.
Brauerei Hönig, Ellerbergstraße 15, 96123 Tiefenellern. **T** 09505 391 www.brauerei-hoenig.de

Untergreuth
Brauerei Büttner is a tiny village brewery, about six kilometres south of Bamberg, but with no public transport connections. It has been in the same family since 1782.

No signs indicate the Gasthaus; the brewery yard serves as a beergarden. There is only one beer, the **Hausbrauer Hell**. Open 17:00 Fridays and from 14:00, Saturdays and Sundays (*only*). **Brauerei Büttner**, Haus no. 8, 96158 Untergreuth. **T** 09502 342

Weiher
This small village, about 10 kilometres from Bamberg doesn't have much to interest a casual visitor apart from the enterprising Brauerei Kundmüller. This is a modern pub with overnight accommodation, with an extensive, attractive garden which backs onto barley fields. **Ungespundete Lagerbier** and **Rauchbier** on draught, and **Pils** and **Weisse** in flip-top bottles comprise the beer selection, and there is also a Schnaps distillery. Closed Wednesdays.
No public transport serves Weiher, but you could walk there from Trabelsdorf or Bischberg.
Brauerei Kundmüller, Haus 13, 96191 Viereth-Trunstadt/ Weiher. **T** 09503 4338 www.kundmueller.de

Würgau
Hartmann is no village local but a fairly upmarket modern hotel and restaurant near Scheßlitz. The restaurant features beer cuisine whilst the brewery at the back produces a fine range of beers including the seasonal **Felsenkeller**, made with whisky malt, and the **Felsentrunk** which has just a hint of conventional smoked malt. The **Erbstrunk 1550** is a black lager commemorating the year of the founding of the brewery. Closed Tuesdays.
Brauerei Hartmann, Fränkische-Schweiz-Straße 26, 96110 Scheßlitz-Würgau. **T** 09542 920300, www.brauerei-hartmann.de

Around Bamberg – pubs in the Landkreis Forchheim, another excellent area for breweries.

Drügendorf

A charming village, which nestles in a fold of the hills of "Franconian Switzerland". Brauerei Gasthof Först is the tap of the Golden Lion brewery and is housed in a lovely old timbered building. The brewery dates from 1525. The old Franconian Lagerbier Is excellent – red-gold in colour and full-flavoured. Closed Thursdays. **Brauerei Först**, Haus 26, 91330 Eggolsheim-Drügendorf. **T** 09545 8583 www.brauerei-foerst.de

Eggolsheim

A small town on the Bamberg-Nürnberg railway line – the town centre is however a fair walk from the station. Here you can find Schwarzes Kreuz, a small brewery with a modernised pub (*closed Wednesdays*). The gold coloured **Vollbier** is served from the wooden barrel and is bitter and full-flavoured. The pleasant tree shaded Keller is only a couple of minutes' walk away. **Brauerei Schwarzes Kreuz** Hauptstraße 33, 91330 Eggolsheim. **T** 09545 8843

Forchheim

A medium sized town on the railway from Bamberg to Nürnberg, with half-timbered buildings and a castle. Four breweries but beware the rather limited opening hours in some of these:

Brauerei Neder, Sattlertorstraße 10, 91301 Forchheim. **T** 09191 2400. Beer served from the wooden barrel, into ceramic mugs. *Open 09:00 to 19:00, Tuesday Ruhetag.*

Brauerei Josef Greif, Serlbacherstraße 10, 91301 Forchheim. **T** 09191 727920 www.brauerei-greif.de. A brewery tap and beergarden where the **Lagerbier** is from the wood. *Opens early, but the opening hours are complex. On Friday, Monday and Wednesday it's open until 22:00, other days it closes at lunchtime.*

Brauerei Eichhorn, Bambergerstraße 9, 91301 Forchheim. **T** 09191 2379 www.gasthaus-eichhorn.de. Forchheim's smallest brewery. The pub, which was built in 1595, has a small garden, **Vollbier** and **Edel-Pils** on draught. *Open from 12:00 (10:00 Saturdays, Sundays and holidays), Tuesday and Wednesday Ruhetag.*

Below: *Forchheim.*

Fritz Hebendanz, Sattlertorstraße 14, 91301 Forchheim. **T** 09191 1222 **www. brauerei-hebendanz.de**. Lovely half-timbered building opposite the old town hall, serving **Export-Hell** beer from wooden barrels.
Open 08:00 to 20:00, 23:00 Friday. Sundays open 13:00 to 20:00. Also closed Thursday afternoons.

The Annafest is one of the largest folk festivals in Franconia, and runs for 10 days from St.Anna's day (July 26th) every year. There are about 20 Kellers (beer gardens) to quench your thirst, featuring the Forchheim breweries and others from the neighbouring area. Most brew a special festival beer at about 5.5 to 6% ABV. Some of the Kellers are open just for the Fest, others open at the usual Keller times. Website: **www.anna-fest.de** or **www.annafest-forchheim.de**

Gunzendorf
The Felsenkeller Senftenberg is a few miles from Buttenheim, signposted as you approach Gunzendorf, and is supplied by the local Sauer brewery. Open from 15:30 at weekends and on public holidays from 13:30. An excellent Keller which has marvellous views.

Hallendorf – Kreuzbergkeller
This is a scenic complex of beer gardens next to a hillside church in woodland near Hallerndorf, which is near Eggolsheim on the Bamberg–Nürnberg railway line. No less than three small local breweries have Kellers here: Rittmayer and Lieberth from Hallerndorf and Friedel from Schnaid. In 2008 Friedel opened a big new replacement Gaststätte here, and this also has a little brewery, to brew special

WALKING TOUR 3
Kreuzbergkeller

From Forchheim station – or the town centre – take the 265 bus. There is quite a reasonable frequency, but none at all on Sundays. This will take you to the centre of Stiebarlimbach and the Roppelt brewery. You then walk north to the Kreuzberg, passing Roppelts Keller, then via a steep path (about one kilometre). After enjoying the Kellers you can walk on to Schnaid (a further kilometre or so) where the 265 will return you to Forchheim. The last bus is just before 18:00. More enthusiastic walkers could start at Eggolsheim station and walk via Schlammersdorf, Trailsdorf and Hallerndorf where there are plenty of refreshment opportunities.

beers for the new pub. You could also try the Brauerei Fischer in nearby Greuth, but it's only open Sunday lunchtimes in summer, although their Keller is open Wednesday to Sunday, again only in summer.

Stiebarlimbach
The Brauerei Roppelt produces an excellent **Kellerbier**, available at their tap in the village (*closed Wednesdays and Thursdays*) and at the Roppelt-Keller, which is open in fine weather at 11:00 except Wednesdays and Thursdays when it opens at 15:30. From the latter it is a steep walk uphill to the Kreuzbergkeller (q.v.).
Brauerei Roppelt, Haus 9, 91352 Hallendorf-Stiebarlimbach.
T 09195 7263
www.brauerei-roppelt.de

Unterzaunsbach
Brauerei Meister is a small village brewery. Those of you who have tried the excellent **Meister Vollbier** (it has appeared at beer festivals in the UK) might want to seek out the brewery tap which is open every day except Tuesday and can be reached weekdays by a bus from Forchheim.
Brauerei Meister, Haus 8, 91362 Pretzfeld-Unterzaunsbach. **T** 09194 9126

A brief beer tour of Franconia

This section does not claim to be a comprehensive survey of Franconia's pubs and breweries, but covers some of the major attractions for beer lovers in the region both in the larger towns and in other places. It also highlights some interesting places for the tourist with or without an interest in beer to visit. If you are serious about exploring Franconia's country pubs and breweries, a copy of Brauns Brauerei Atlas or CAMRA's *Good Beer Guide Germany*, and a good local map are essential.

With careful planning, taking note of rest days and opening hours, you could enjoy many walking or cycling tours to explore Franconia.

Franconia – an introduction

Franconia takes its name from the Frankish tribes that once settled the region; at one time it extended as far west as Mainz and the Rhine. Although Franconia has long been incorporated into Bavaria, its people see themselves as Franconian rather than Bavarian. Franconia makes up the northern half of Bavaria, and extends from Aschaffenburg, Würzburg and the Romantic Road in the west to Bayreuth in the east and from Coburg and Hof in the north to Nürnberg and Ansbach in the south.

Superficially, Franconia appears to comprise mainly rolling hills and sombre forests, without any spectacular natural features. However there are many distinct geographical regions and nine different national parks. Much of Franconia is rural and given over to agriculture, but there are many reminders of the past in its romantic castles and fortresses.

Bad Windsheim

From Bamberg you might wish to visit the historic town of Rothenburg ob der Tauber, if so you can follow the "Aisch valley beer trail" for the first part of your journey by road, calling at this pleasant little country town. Here the Brauhaus Döbler has an old fashioned taproom where you can try the unfiltered Reichstadtbier and the Löschauer Dunkel. Closed Sundays and Tuesday from noon. The other brewery in the town, Bürgerbräu, ceased brewing in 2001.

Bad Windsheim has the Fränkische Freilandmuseum, which features three historic brewery buildings that have been reconstructed on this site. Two of these breweries are now in working order and produce occasional brews. Open Mid-March to November, closed Mondays.

Details of the beer trail – which also offers a three day "beer experience" are on www.bierstrasse.de which has a substantial English version. Worth investigating if you want to explore some of the lesser-known beers of Franconia.

Bayreuth

The home of the annual Richard Wagner opera festivals, held at the Festspielhaus designed by Wagner himself. Despite the international fame of the festival, Bayreuth remains a pleasantly old-fashioned place with much to offer not only to the opera buff but to the sightseer and beer-drinker as well. There are now only three operating breweries.

Becherbräu, a fair walk from the city centre in St.Nikolaus Straße, is a good, old-fashioned brewery tap with nice displays of old beer mugs. You can try Vollbier and a very cloudy "Naturtrübes Kraüsenpils" on draught. There is also a winter Bock. Tuesday is Ruhetag.

Glenk, which is not far from Becher, has no proper tap, only a summer beer garden at its brewery in Eichelweg, although their beer can be found in pubs around the town.

Maisel is one of the biggest breweries in Franconia and is internationally known for its Maisel's Weisse, although other beers are produced for the local market, and their Dampfbier made a welcome reappearance about six years ago. It is still in the ownership of the Maisel family. Maisel's "Brauerei und Büttnereimuseum" has been set up in the former brewery (next door to the modern plant) and preserves the original brewhouse of 1874 and a cooper's workshop. A fascinating display, from the massive steam engines down to the huge collections of glasses and mugs. It appeared in the Guinness Book of Records in 1988 as the largest brewery museum in the world in terms of floor space. Open Mondays to Saturdays at 10:00 but group tours can be booked at other times. The museum is in Kulmbacher Strasse 40, **T** 0921 401234. Next door is the Maisel brewery tap, the Goldener Löwe at Kulmbacher Straße 30 (*Closed Tuesdays and on Sundays from 14:00*), which also offers accommodation.

Other pubs worth a visit are Brauerei-schänke Am Markt in Maximillian Straße, which boasts a "Zwick'l Bier" speciality from the Bayreuther Bierbrauerei which the author found to be very tasty, red gold in colour, and with low carbonation. The beer is brewed by Maisel. The Schinner Braustuben, the former Schinner brewery tap in Richard Wagner Straße has Alt Bayreuther Braunbier and Meistersinger Pils on draught. The beers are said to be brewed at Kaiser of Neuhaus a.d. Pegnitz. Tuesday Ruhetag.

Burgkunstadt
Until recently Burgkunstadt had four home-brew pubs all conveniently located in the centre of this picturesque village, which is on the railway line between Bamberg and Kulmbach. Alas, all but one – Günther-Bräu – have now ceased brewing.

Coburg
Coburg has strong links with the British Royal family; Prince Albert, Queen Victoria's consort, grew up at the Ehrenburg castle. The imposing fortress (Veste), one of the largest in Germany, is a highlight in an attractive town which is well worth exploring. The town's Scheidmantel and Erste Coburger Exportbrauerei (Sturm) breweries were both taken over by the Kulmbacher group in 2002. It seems that brewing continues at Sturm with the beers marketed together under the Coburg Brauerei name.

Erlangen
A university town, known for its baroque architecture. It is home to the famous Erlangen Bergkirchweih, a twelve-day church festival at Whitsuntide, celebrated at the beergardens above the town. Kitzmann is the local brewery, and its beer can be found widely in the town, although there is no tap as such. It was joined by the Steinbach Bräu brew-pub in 1995.

Heckenhof
Käthi-Bräu is a rustic country pub, founded in 1498, near Aufseß (about 25 kilometres east of Bamberg, occasional buses) with a black lager as its sole product. Popular with motor-cyclists, this pub has plenty of outside seating.

Herzogenaurach
The small country brewery of Hans Heller is situated in a village in the Aurach valley and produces some splendid Franconian brews, including an aromatic unfiltered Pils that is far removed from British ersatz lagers. Its bottled beers have delightful labels. The Hellerbräu pub closes at 13:00 Thursdays and Sundays, and closes for a midday break (*13:00 to 15:00*) on other days. Bus 201 from Erlangen.

Kloster Kreuzberg

This is the only monastery brewery in Franconia, located about 100 kilometres north-west of Bamberg, in the mountainous region of the Rhön. Franciscan monks have brewed here since 1731. It's reminiscent of the far more commercial and crowded Kloster Andechs near Munich. To get there, follow the B279 to Bischofsheim from where directions are sign-posted clearly. Kloster Kreuzberg comprises a large complex of monastery buildings, and the Klosterschenke has a number of rooms for drinking as well as an extensive outside drinking area. There is self service for food and the excellent dark beer (Bock beer in season). Please note it closes at 20:00 daily and is closed November to mid-December. There is also a hotel with a restaurant, and a separate pub sells Karmeliten beer from a secular brewery in nearby Bad Neustadt.

Kronach

An attractive fortified hilltop town in the north of Franconia, with a rail link to Bamberg. The local beer is Kaiserhof, and their Pils and the dark Schwedentrunk (which reflects the links with the Thirty Years' War) can be drunk at the Burgschänke on the terrace of the castle, which has magnificent views over the town, and the Kaiserhof pub at the brewery in Friesener Straße (*closed Mondays*) in the town.

Kulmbach

Until recently, Kulmbach, a small town with only around 30,000 inhabitants, boasted five large breweries, producing over two million hectolitres of beer a year and supplying beer nationally and for export. Kulmbach has a brewing history akin to Munich rather than other towns in Upper Franconia such as Bamberg, Bayreuth or Coburg. It established itself as a supplier of Bavarian beer in the mid-nineteenth century and its breweries' range of beers never encompassed the local Franconian styles. However it was particularly known for its dark and strong beers. The EKU 28 was a contender for the strongest beer in the world, with a gravity of 28 degrees and an alcohol content of over 13.5 percent, and EKU's Kulminator was a powerful dark Doppelbock. Reichelbräu's Eisbock Bayrisch G'frorns was an example of an ice beer where the alcohol is concentrated by freezing. *Kulmbacher* became a registered trade mark.

In recent years the Kulmbach breweries have suffered major upheavals. Schweizerhof, which was the first to become part of a major national German brewing group, fell victim to the Sailer group's rationalisation plans and closed in 1992. The rest are now part of the Kulmbacher Brauerei group, the eleventh largest brewing group in Germany. Sandlerbrau merged with Reichelbräu in 1995 and the Ersten Kulmbacher Actienbrauerei (EKU), once part of the defunct Marz group, was bought by Reichelbräu who by this time also part-owned Mönchshof.

All the beers are now produced in one high-tech brewery. The ranges of beers have been rationalised but not as drastically as might be expected. The Kulmbacher Brauerei group also own three breweries in the former East Germany, and is now owned by Brau Holding International which in turn is part of the Heineken empire.

The name Reichelbräu has disappeared but a range of seven beers under the Kulmbacher label include the famous Eisbock, the alcoholic content of which was for a while rather lower than the original but has now been restored to 9.2%. EKU survives as a range of five beers in long necked bottles, plus the EKU 28 which weighs in at 11% ABV.

Mönchshof was the oldest brewery in Kulmbach, originating as a monastery brewery in 1349. Its best known product, Kloster Schwarz-Bier continued the monastic brewing tradition and was the most well-known example of the traditional dark beers of Kulmbach. For a time it was marketed as the "Black Pils". Mönchshof Schwarzbier is still included in a range of six beers produced under the Mönchshof label and bottled in swing-top bottles. Seven types of wheat beer are produced under the old Mönchshof Kapuziner label.

Despite the changes above, Kulmbach is still promoted as the "beer city" and the annual beer week still takes place. This is an annual festival rivalling Munich's Oktoberfest and runs from the last Saturday in July for nine days. The centre of the town is given over to huge tents in which drinkers are entertained by bands.

You will be disappointed if you are looking for quaint brewery taps in Kulmbach; the big brewers here established large pub-restaurants and it is difficult to find "pubby" establishments to enjoy the beers. Mönchshof Bräuhaus is the former Mönchshof brewery, a large complex of buildings outside the town at Hofer Straße 20, is now a pub and restaurant with a large beer garden, which is open from 10:00 daily but closed Mondays. There is a brewery museum, open daily 10:00 to 17:00 with a small brewery which produces beer for the pub.

Kulmbach also has a relatively new brewery enterprise in the form of the Kulmbacher Kommunbräu which opened in 1994 at Grünwehr 17. Closed Tuesdays.

Kulmbach is an attractive town with many historic buildings in its compact centre. A "toy" train (Bimmelbahn) which runs on the roadway will take you from the centre up the steep hill to the massive Plassenberg fortress, where the Deutsche Zinnfigurenmuseum displays the world's largest collection of miniature tin figures.

Neuhaus an der Pegnitz
Easily reached from Nuremberg by train (30 minute journey, trains every hour). This is of interest t o all beer lovers because of its Zoigl tradition (see below). Three families brew at the communal brewhouse, which dates back to 1556. They take it in turn to sell their Märzen style beer – the change is made every three weeks. The participating families are:

GEORG DÖTH, Burgstrasse
PAUL REINDL, Unterer Markt
PAUL BENABURGER, Unterer Markt

Each pub opens from 08:00. There is a Kirchweih on the first Sunday in October on which day all four pubs are open. Neuhaus is also home to the large Kaiser Bräu brewery whose beers can be sampled at the Hotel Burg Veldenstein, the brewery tap at the Veldenstein castle (closed Mondays).

Nürnberg (Nuremberg)
The largest city in Franconia, with a population of over half a million, Nürnberg was one of the best-preserved mediaeval townscapes in Europe. Following wartime destruction the city has been lovingly reconstructed and contains much of interest – the churches of St. Sebald, St. Lorenz and the Frauenkirche, the patrician houses, and the imperial castle that towers over the inner city. The narrow streets below the castle and by the city walls are particularly atmospheric.

Tourists flock to the Christmas market or Christkindlmarkt held in Nürnberg over the weeks leading up to Christmas. Amongst the delicacies on offer is Lebkuchen, the local gingerbread, which even has its own website. Nürnberg's Christmas market is one of the biggest and best-known in Germany, but many other towns have a similar event, including Bamberg.

Until fairly recently, Nürnberg had two large breweries, Tucher and Patrizier, whose beers were widely available both in the city and in Franconia as a whole. Now there is just Tucher and the Patrizier name has virtually disappeared. Patrizier was a relatively modern product of the mergers and rationalisation of several brewery companies in the area, but did once brew a Rauchbier and Altes-Kupfer, an unfiltered red beer. The Tuchers were one of the old patrician families of Nürnberg and their brewing history goes back to 1672. They now actually brew in the neighbouring town of Fürth, which is part of the Nürnberg conurbation.

Contrasting sharply with the above is the tiny Hausbrauerei Altstadthof in the heart of the old city at Bergstraße 18. It was established in May 1984 and at the time it was the

first new brewery to be established in Bavaria for a quarter of a century. It was designed to brew a naturally conditioned organic beer reviving old techniques. It now has a range of beers. A kiosk sells the beers in one litre flip-top bottles and there are other products including beer mustards.

More recently Altstadthof has been joined by two more brewpubs as well as several pubs that specialise in beers from the country breweries around Nürnberg.

Nürnberg has a thriving nightlife and there are hundreds of eating and drinking places, including plenty of traditional-style Franconian pubs and of course the sausage restaurants which specialise in the small spicy Nürnberg sausages (Rostbratwürste), usually sold in multiples of three or four and accompanied by sauerkraut, bread, beer and mustard. These restaurants have a good atmosphere and should be tried, but don't expect to find anything exciting in the way of beer. The Röslein on Rathausplatz is as good as any, fast food Franconian-style with a range of Tucher beers to wash it down. Others can be found at www.die-nuernberger-bratwurst.de.

A downside is that in contrast to the rest of Franconia, the beer drinker will find "big city"

prices In Nürnberg – a half-litre of beer is usually at least €1 dearer here than in Bamberg.

Every June there is a Franconian beer festival (Fränkische Bierfest) in the moat of the castle where many of Franconia's favourite country breweries are represented. Unfortunately there is no website for this event.

There is a good integrated transport system in the city, including a 15-minute U-Bahn connection to the airport. The ticket machines have instructions in English. A 24-hour ticket enabling unlimited travel around the city can be purchased, and there is also a "city card" which gives unrestricted use of public transport and access to more than 30 museums, plus a guided tour. The tourist office is opposite the main station **T** 0911 2336 123 www.nuernberg.de.

www.museen.nuernberg.de is a website for the many museums in the city, which include a museum of wheat beer glasses! Of more general interest are the Transport Museum and the German National museum, the latter with comprehensive displays of paintings, sculptures and other works of art. The city's connection with the Third Reich is still something today's citizens have to live with. The Nazis chose Nürnberg because of its symbolic links with mediaeval Germany, and their annual rallies were held here. Things came full circle with the destruction of the old city in a massive air raid and the subsequent post-war trials of the Nazi leaders, which took place at the Palace of Justice. The buildings and parade ground of the Nazi era can still be seen at the Luitpoldhain, south east of the city centre. A new museum now sensitively documents this era – the Dokumentationszentrum Reichsparteitagsgelände at Bayernstrasse 110.

Every November Nürnberg hosts Brau Beviale, a trade fair for the beverage industry at the city's exhibition grounds (Messe). Over 1300 exhibitors – mainly associated with the brewing industry – take part and over 34,000 people attended in 2008 (there was no fair in 2009).

Nürnberg pub listings

Hausbrauerei Barfüßer, Hallplatz 2
Open 11:00 to midnight
Brew pub established in 1994 in the basement of the ancient Mauthaus. One of the new generation of German microbreweries, it produces unfiltered **Blonde** and **Schwarze** beers and is advertised as "small brewery, big experience". It follows that the brewhouse itself is very small (and sited in the bar) and the pub is very large. The attractive vaulted basement room is traditionally decorated with only the hanging British pub signs looking somewhat out of place.

Café Express, Bulmann Straße 4
Open 11:00 weekdays, 12:00 Saturdays, 15:00 Sundays, to 01:00.
Bamberg and country beers on draught, also features live music.

Kloster Andechs – das Wirtshaus (formerly Der Andechser) in Deutscher Kaiser Hotel, Königstraße 55. *Open 11:00 to midnight*
Fount for the monastic brewery near Munich with all their beers featured, at least four on draught.

Hütt'n, Burgstraße 19
Opens 16:00 weekdays, 11:00 weekends.
Closes for a summer holiday, so check the website www.huettn-nuernberg.de
The "little mountain hut" is recommended for its country beer specialities, and has a good selection of draught and bottled beers including a house beer from Fischer of Greuth. Don't confuse the address with that of Schwarzer Bauer below.

Landbierparadies ("country beer paradise")
This chain has four branches at Wodanstraße 15 (can be walked from the south exit of the main station or U Bahn station Maffeiplatz), Rothenburger Straße 26 (near U Bahn station Plärrer, Sterzinger Straße 4–6, and Galvanistraße 10, plus another in Fürth. All the pubs have a daily guest draught beer from a Franconian country brewery plus a selection of bottles. At all the pubs the opening pattern seems to be 17:00 to late, with lunchtime opening only at weekends and public holidays. A beer shop at Galgenhofstraße 60 is owned by the same people and is open on Monday to Friday from 10:00 to 18:30, and on Saturday from 09:00 to 16:00.

Lederer Biersiederei, Sielstraße 12
Open 10:00 to midnight (01:00 Fridays and Saturdays)
The former brewery tap of the Lederer brewery, with a large beer garden, situated near the U-Bahn station Bärenschanze. Lederer beers are now brewed by Tucher but the crocodile trademark is still a familiar sight around the city. Casks of Lederer beer were the first freight to be transported on German railways, following the opening of the line from Nürnberg to Fürth in 1836. At Lederer you can drink **Kroko**, a "spezial Kellerbier", and admire the artefacts in the bar which include a brewery steam engine and inevitably, a giant crocodile.

Schwarzer Bauer, Bergstraße 19–21
Open 11:00 to 01:00
Tap for the tiny Altstadthof brewery next door. A busy little bar where the locals drink the **Helles**, **Schwarze**, **Rothes** (a traditional local red beer) and **Weisse** beers with great gusto. The Musikkeller Schmelztiegel next door opens 19:00 and also features Altstadthof beers.

Singularis Porcus, Harsdörfferstraße 8
Open 19:00 to 01:00. Pub and beer garden with Franconian country beer a speciality.

Schanzenbräu, Adam-Klein Straße 27
New brewery in Nürnberg-Gostenhof, supplying a number of other bars with its **Rot** and **Hell** beers. Its tap is called the Schankwirtschaft. *Opens 17:00, 11:00 on Sundays.*

Gasthaus Schranke (Schlenkerla),
Tiergärtnertor 3. *Open 11:00 to 23:00. closed Sundays.*
Right in the centre of the old city by the Albrecht-Dürer-Haus. A good choice of beers here, including **Schlenkerla** from Bamberg. The right to use the Schlenkerla name was granted many years ago.

Gasthaus Schranke (Schlenkerla), Nuremberg.

Tucherbräu Stüberl, Am Kartäusertor 1
Open 10:00 to midnight
Showpiece for the Tucher brewery.

Zunftstübchen, Am Olberg 35
An old rambling building by the castle,
with precipitous stairways, dating from 1678.
There is a pleasant outside drinking area and
Kitzmann beer from Erlangen.

Other local breweries represented in Nuremberg are Zirndorf, Wolfshöhe and Weißenoher
Klosterbier. St.Georgen from Buttenheim is
available at Böhm's Herrenskeller, Theater-
gasse 19 and Zum Sudhaus, Bergstraße 20,
the latter being a famous gastronomic venue
much visited by the rich and famous!

Pottenstein

Situated in a picturesque gorge in "Franconian
Switzerland", Pottenstein is overshadowed
by an imposing castle and is famous for the
nearby Teufelshöhle caves. Pottenstein can
be reached by bus from Pegnitz which in turn
is on the railway service from Nurnberg to
Bayreuth. Its two pub breweries are easily
found on the high street. Brauerei Hufeisen is
a quiet pub with a classic **Franconian Urdunkel**,

dark and bitter, served from the wooden barrel.
Monday is Ruhetag. Brauereigasthof Mager is
a lovely old building, although the interior is
fairly standard. The full range of beers includes
a **Dunkel**, which is an excellent and very dark
beer. The author thought this reminiscent of
a British old ale, and also the best in town!
There is accommodation. What was once the
Brauereigasthof of the Wagner brewery still
carries the old name but its official name is the
Frankenland Stuben – unfortunately brewing
ceased a few years ago. It has a genuinely old
Franconian style interior, and the **Pottensteiner
Höhlentrunk** beer comes from St.Georgen.

Rothenburg ob der Tauber

The Brauerei Gasthof Landwehrbräu is a fairly
upmarket complex of brewery, hotel and restaurant at Reichelshofen, a few kilometres from
the famous old mediaeval town of Rothenburg.
The modern brewery produces a fine range of
beers and the half-timbered buildings provide
a most attractive setting in which to enjoy them.

Staffelstein

A picturesque town in the Main valley, where
the attractions include the half-timbered town
hall, fortifications, and streams that rush
under the streets. There is a good selection of
pubs but all the town's five home-brew houses
ceased brewing in the last 15 years. However
Staffelberg-Bräu in nearby Loffeld is worth a
visit. In Staffelstein itself, Gasthof Adam Riese
is a pub with beer from **Schwanen Bräu** of
nearby Ebensfeld. Adam Riese was a mathe-
matician who lived in Staffelstein. Near Staffelstein, on the slopes above the river Main, is
Kloster Banz, the former Benedictine abbey;
on the other side of the valley is the pilgrimage
church of Vierzehnheiligen (q.v.)

Vierzehnheiligen

A few kilometres from Staffelstein, the Brauerei
Trunk is situated next to the famous pilgrimage
church of the 14 saints of the intercession and
its brewery tap caters for walkers and pilgrims.
There is a pub, the Klosterbräustübchen with a
beergarden, which is self-service with a deposit

on the mugs. Otherwise the beer can be drunk at the large, touristy Zum Stern which is geared for coach parties, and is next to a rather tacky complex of souvenir shops. Excellent **"Nothelfer-Trunk"**, a rich and distinctive medium-dark Vollbier.

Würzburg

A wonderful baroque city on the river Main, Würzburg is the capital of "wine Franconia", and is said to have banned brewing for ever in the 14th century. The vineyards clinging to the slopes above the river confirm that even today wine dominates – there are numerous wine restaurants and the distinctive Frankenwein can also be sampled at the cellars of the various wine merchants. However, beer lovers need not despair. The former court brewery, Würzburger Hofbräu, has a large pub and beer garden (the Hofbräukeller at Höchberger Strasse 28, but is now part of the Heineken empire. There is also a microbrewery, the Fränkische Brauhaus am Spitäle at Burkaderstraße 2–4, which was established in 1989.

The quest for the Zoigl

If Kellerbier and Rauchbier reflect old brewing styles, the Zoigl goes back even further, to mediaeval times when brewing rights were granted to individuals in return for payment of taxes. Although individuals granted this privilege can brew at home, brewing usually takes place at communal brewhouses owned by the community or by an association of home brewers. A peripatetic brewer takes charge of the brewing operation, and the participants take away the wort for fermentation and lagering on their own premises.

When the beer is ready to serve the Zoigl or six-pointed star is hung outside their premises. The word Zoigl seems to derive from "Zeichen", the German word for sign, and the Zoigl star was the sign used by brewers in the Middle Ages.

This tradition continues at a number of locations in East Franconia and in the neighbouring Oberpfalz (or Upper Palatinate), the far eastern part of Bavaria, for years isolated up against the closed borders with Czechoslovakia. In the Oberpfalz communal brewing was once very common with over 75 towns having a communal brewery in the mid-nineteenth century. The Zoigl outlets in the Oberpfalz are not pubs and do not open pub hours, neither is Zoigl beer sold in pubs. At the appointed time, the Zoigl brewers hang out the sign and open a room in their house to sell the beer; in some towns they take it in turns. The Zoigl brewers of the Oberpfalz maintain that the Franconian version is not a true Zoigl and indeed in Neuhaus-Pegnitz, the "Zoigl" is produced by pub owners using a communal brewhouse. Seßlach is another Franconian town with two pubs using a communal brewhouse.

Apparently there is now even a commercially produced Zoigl beer but it is difficult to see how this can stand comparison with the real thing.

Today the Zoigl tradition is enjoying something of a revival, but it is still surrounded by mystery and hard to find, mainly because of the lack of published information and secrecy surrounding the outlets. Combined with the characteristic local reluctance found in this part of the world, where pubs don't really seem to want to advertise their existence let alone their opening hours, and tend to open and close on a whim anyway! But the Zoigl is becoming less of a mystery, and judging by the websites, something of a cult following is developing! See also www.zoigl.de which is an English-language site.

Information on Zoigl brewers at Windischeschenbach and Neuhaus in the Oberpfalz (not to be confused with Neuhaus a.d. Pegnitz in Franconia) can be found at www.zoiglbier.de; this includes a calendar detailing who will be selling the Zoigl. Other towns with Zoigl brewers in the Oberpfalz are Falkenberg, Eslarn and Mitterteich.

Regional food and non-beer drinks

In the morning, strolling around the city of Bamberg, you cannot fail to notice delicious smells of smoked bacon, onions, grilled sausages, roast knuckles of pork, sauerkraut and rich spiced red cabbage hanging in the air. Lunch is being prepared.

It is futile to pretend that the local cuisine is anything but wholesome, tasty and filling. It doesn't plumb any gastronomic depths, but local chefs are developing a somewhat lighter touch, and outside influences are becoming more evident, particularly pasta and Italian dishes.

The main meal is eaten at midday when you might find special dishes of the day (Tagesgerichte) and menus of the day (Tagesmenu). The latter will offer a good value meal of soup with main course and even a token dessert – otherwise, desserts are rarely served in the traditional pubs. There may be special dishes for children (Kinderteller) and senior citizens (Seniorenteller), which will involve smaller portions than the generous norm.

Food shopping

Bamberg's market takes place every day except Sundays and holidays in the main square (Maxplatz) and offers superb quality local fruit and vegetables, as well as other delicacies. Much of this is the product of the local market gardening industry, which is still going strong. It has to be said that this fine produce isn't much in evidence on menus in local pubs, which do not tend to offer much in the way of vegetable dishes. On Saturday mornings there is also a farmer's market at the northern end of Promenadestraße.

Local butchers and charcuteries put Britain's supermarket counters to shame with their beautifully presented and extensive selections of meats, all served in scrupulously clean surroundings. Also admirable are the bakeries and pastry shops, again outstanding in their high standards and variety.

There are several small (by UK or US standards) supermarkets in the centre of Bamberg. As in the rest of Germany shop opening hours are somewhat limited and only fairly recently have bakers been permitted to bake on Sundays!

Local menus

Most traditional pubs provide reasonably priced meals and snacks – solid, tasty Franconian fare. This usually stakes its claim to be "gut Bürgerliche Küche" – good home cooking, even though it might be noticed that some modern catering shortcuts are creeping in. Dishes may be titled "Hausfrau Art" (housewife style) or "Grossmütter Art" (grandma's style). Kitchens, even in the most remote and rustic old country pub will be up-to-date and resplendent in stainless steel, with staff immaculately turned out in whites. However some country pubs may only provide hot food (Germans always refer to "hot" food as "warm" food) on Sundays and holidays.

Menus can be pretty daunting to the non-German speaker. Even those with a basic knowledge of German will have problems, because menus contain dialect words and local specialities as well as the inevitable compounded words, beloved of the Germans. The best advice for the latter is to divide them up into the component words – as if you were cutting up a big Wurst! Also confusing are the different names under which similar dishes can appear in different restaurants. Given that German food is seldom seen in Britain, I have set out some explanation of the commonly found menu items. Most traditional places will not have an English menu; beware such translations as do occasionally appear, although the intention is good, they will probably leave you even more confused!

Soups and starters

To start, most menus will list a few hearty soups, but rarely any other starters. Some are based on a clear soup or broth for example Leberknödelsuppe (with liver dumplings) or Pfannkuchensuppe (with pancake strips). Others are thick and moreish, such as Serbische Bohnensuppe (Serbian bean), Gulaschsuppe or Erbsensuppe (pea).

Meat dishes

Menus are dominated by pork meat. Beef and veal are also popular, but chicken less so compared to the UK, and lamb is relatively uncommon on menus.

Many pubs have their own slaughter-house and butchery and you might find a "slaughter plate" on the menu. The traditional peasant ceremony of slaughtering the pig is followed by tremendous industry by family and friends to turn every part of the unfortunate beast into a huge variety of sausages, ham, brawn and other products. What is not consumed immediately is preserved or smoked to provide food for the months to come. The range of pork charcuterie for which this region is renowned reflects this variety of pork meats – cold, hot, cooked, smoked and cured.

Snacks/Brotzeit

It is impossible to render the exact sense of Brotzeit in English, literally "bread time" this is a substantial snack to go with beer, often eaten mid-morning. Pub snacks are substantial and as in Germany generally, pubs do not sell the crisps, nuts, pork scratchings etc that are beloved of the British beer drinker. You will see the occasional machine that dispenses peanuts. Schmankerl is a word used locally for a snack menu.

Pretzels (in local dialect Brezen), are not the hard little things that come in packets and choke American presidents, but large rings of soft fresh bread. Popular at festivals, but sometimes you might find them as a snack in pubs.

Sausages

If beer is Germany's national drink, its cuisine is epitomised by Wurst. The German sausage comes in many varieties, cooked and uncooked, hot and cold, sliced and whole. Every region of Germany has its own favourite sausages and Franconia is no exception.

Bratwurst are the most common, being served grilled or fried. Nürnberger Bratwurst are small and spicy, grilled and sold in multiples of three. They are traditionally cooked over a charcoal grill in Nuremberg's sausage restaurants, but can be found on menus throughout Franconia. Bratwurst from Coburg are also very highly regarded.

Bockwurst or the larger Knackwurst are what we call a Frankfurter or hot dog sausage, smoked and poached in hot water.

British lovers of Indian food needn't get excited over Currywurst – this is a large grilled sausage served with a dollop of tomato ketchup with some curry powder shaken over.

Blaue Zipfel is a local speciality – Bratwurst poached with onions, vinegar, juniper berries and bay leaf.

Pork (Schweinefleisch)

Schweinebraten – roast pork, also found in the following variants:

Schäuferla – "Little spade" – a joint from the shoulder.

Spiessbraten – a joint roasted on a spit
Schweinshaxe – a dauntingly large knuckle of pork, often served with beer gravy and called *Bierhaxe*, or grilled on a spit (*Grillhaxe*).

All roasts are invariably served with gravy and dumplings.

Knöchla – a similarly large boiled knuckle of bacon, known as Eisbein in northern Germany.
Schweineschnitzel "Wiener Art" – the plain pork schnitzel fried in breadcrumbs. *Jägerschnitzel* is cooked in a mushroom sauce, *Zigeunerschnitzel* with peppers, onion and tomato, and *Schnitzel Cordon Bleu* with ham and cheese.
Schweinefilet – fillet of pork or medallions, maybe served in a cream and mushroom sauce (champignonrahmsosse).
Schweinelendchen – pork loin steaks.
Schweinekotelett – pork chop.

To confuse you further dishes might be described as *Schnitzel vom Schwein* (from the pig) rather than *Schweineschnitzel*! Or a *Jägerschnitzel* might be described as a *Schnitzel nach Jäger Art* (hunter style)!

Spanferkel – suckling pig, usually served roasted.
Kasseler – a smoked and cured bacon cutlet.

Beef *(Rindfleisch)* and Veal *(Kalb)*
Except in the basic Gaststätte, the usual beefsteak dishes are available e.g *Rumpsteak, Pfeffersteak* etc., but are at the top end of the menu, price-wise. A favourite local beef dish is *Sauerbraten* – a pot roast with a slight "sweet and sour" flavour, the meat having been marinated in wine or vinegar. Also found on menus is *Ochsenbrust mit Meerrettich* – beef with horseradish, and *Rinderroulade*, a rolled and stuffed loaf of minced beef.

Veal may form the basis of roast and schnitzel dishes similar to pork.

Deutsches Beefsteak – a pretentious name for a hamburger.
Hackbraten – a meat loaf.

Leberkäs – a pork and beef loaf, nothing to do with liver or cheese! Very popular as a hot snack with bread and mustard.

Other meats
Hähnchen – chicken. The dialect word "*Göggerla*" is sometimes used.
Truthahn or Pute – turkey. Noticeably more common on menus in recent years, as a "healthy" substitute for pork.
Ente – duck
Gans – goose, the traditional German Christmas dish.

Offal is also popular, you might find liver (*Leber*), kidneys (*Nieren*), tripe (*Fleck*) and lights (*Lunge*). *Kuttel* is a stew of offal and can contain all sorts of unmentionable parts of the animal!

Fish
There does not tend to be a huge variety available, given the distance of this region from the sea. *Matjes*, the pickled herring or rollmop, as in all Germany, is a favourite snack. Farmed freshwater carp and trout from local fisheries are popular when in season. At festival time, the pungent smell of grilled mackerel and herring is a popular addition to the atmosphere!

Accompaniments
In this region of Germany, main dishes are often served with the big potato dumplings known as *Kloß*, or less frequently with bread dumplings (*Semmelkloß*). Other accompaniments include *Spätzle* (home-made noodles), *Reis* (rice) or potatoes. The latter are served in a variety of ways:
Salzkartoffeln (steamed*)*, *Petersilienkartoffeln* (with parsley*)*, *Kroketten, Kartoffelpuree or Kartoffelbrei* (mashed*)*, *Bratkartoffeln* (fried) or as *Pommes Frites*. Potato salad, which is unfortunately often bought in ready prepared rather than home-made is also a very popular accompaniment to both hot and cold dishes.

Cabbage closely rivals the potato as the national vegetable of Germany. *Sauerkraut* (often abbreviated to *Kraut* on menus) is shredded white cabbage, packed into barrels and pickled. It varies considerably in sharpness

67

and sweetness and according to the spices added.

Red cabbage (*Rotkohl*) is the type of cabbage most commonly served, cooked without vinegar it becomes "blue cabbage" (*Blaukraut*). Local green cabbage (*Wirsing*), cooked to a puree, is a popular summer accompaniment.

Most main course dishes will come with a small side salad containing sometimes more preserved vegetables than fresh, in a sour cream or vinaigrette dressing.

Cold meats

These are some of the more commonly found types that will feature on a "slaughter plate" or as part of "Brotzeit" and as such are staple fare at the Kellers:

Schinken – ham, served either roher (raw i.e. cured) or gekocht (cooked)

Zwetschgenbames – thin slices of beef smoked over plum wood, a local speciality.

Dosenfleisch – literally "tinned flesh", a generic name for cooked sausages that are sliced for serving.

Göttinger – a large sliced sausage, served cold

Weisser Pressack – a brawn sausage, served cold.

Roter Pressack – black pudding or blood sausage

Sülze – brawn

Rauchfleisch – smoked bacon.

Speck – equivalent to British bacon or pancetta, often used cubed (lardoons) in cooking.

Salads and "plates"

Salads are served in the style of the French "salade composée", already dressed. The most straightforward snack item is a platter of cheese or ham served with bread – usually slices of the close-textured brown Landbrot, butter and some salad garnish only.

Wurstsalat is likely to be a sliced cold sausage served *"mit Musik"* – with vinaigrette and raw onion, accompanied by black bread. Strong stuff! "Muzik" is an allusion to the flatulent effect of the onions!

Seasonal dishes and Game

The arrival of seasonal dishes is much anticipated by local people. Carp is in season in the months with an "r", the valley of the river Aisch in particular being famous for this fish. Traditionally the carp is fried whole in batter, but can be served "blue". Asparagus (Spargel) arrives in the markets in June, when restaurants and pubs will offer a special menu of dishes, similarly with chanterelle mushrooms (*Pfifferlinge*) from August onwards. Other wild mushrooms will be on the menus in Autumn along with a variety of game dishes (*Wild*) including venison, hare and wild boar from the Franconian forests.

Vegetarian food

It's not a good place for vegetarians, although things are improving as the range of cuisine expands and outside influences impact on even the most traditional eating places. It is still necessary to be careful of "vegetarian" dishes that contain meat. "Kloß und Soß" is sometimes offered, this is merely dumplings with gravy, and it would be wise to check if the latter is meat-based. *Zwiebelkuchen* is an onion tart reminiscent of Alsace.

Cheese

Despite the strong smells that emanate from supermarket counters and the specialist stalls, German cheeses are often quite bland in taste, and there are few hard cheeses of the British type. *Gerupfter* is frequently found on menus. It is a rich mixture of curd cheese, Camembert, onions, butter and paprika, similar to the Bavarian *Obatz'n*. *Zwiebeleskäs* is home-made curd cheese or Quark with herbs.

Breakfast

This follows the usual continental pattern. In addition to rolls (*Semmeln* or *Brötchen*) you might be served the local speciality *Bamberger Hörnchen* (little horns), a type of croissant. There will usually be some sliced meats and cheese, and perhaps an egg which is likely to be somewhere between soft and hard-boiled, and lukewarm.

Takeaways

Takeaway food has not been developed here in the same way as in the UK and USA, although MacDonalds and Burger King are represented in Bamberg. During the day sources of fast food are the snack counters (Imbiss) or the mobile sausage stands that operate in market places or at fairs. Decent filled rolls can be bought from bakers, delicatessens and fish-mongers. Bakers often have a small stand-up eating area where you can have a coffee and one of the speciality local cakes for example the open plum tarts made with the small, dark local plums (*Zwetschgen*).

Turkish cafes offer various kebabs to take away at all hours, and you will sometimes find snacks such as Schashlik that originate in the former Yugoslavia. Chinese and Indian restaurants do not offer a takeout service. Incidentally, there only appears to be one Indian restaurant in Bamberg, the relatively new Tadsch Mahal at Nurnbergerstrasse 125.

Beer cuisine

Beer is used frequently in cooking and anyone interested in exploring local beer cuisine can find a selection of traditional recipes on the St.Georgen brewery website (www.kellerbier.de).

Other drinks

Schnaps

A spirit distilled from grain or fruit, with about 40% of alcohol. Chasing beer with Schnaps is not recommended unless you are used to this German tradition. Besides the national brands, you will find that many small breweries in Franconia also distill their own Schnaps from local fruit (Obstler), or from a specific fruit e.g. Himbeer, Zwetschgen (local dark plums), Mirabelle (small yellow plums), Apfel, Schlehen (sloe) Williams Birnen or Williams Christ (pear), Quitten (quince), Weintraubenschnaps (grape) etc.

Breweries (including Mahrs and Schlenkerla) also produce Bierschnapps, distilled from beer.

Home-distilled liqueurs (Liköre) are also produced, these have about 20% of alcohol.

Frankenwein

To the west of Bamberg lies the wine producing area of Franconia, extending from Zeil am Main west along the Main valley to Würzburg and beyond. Frankenwein is rarely exported to the UK and is little known outside Germany. The main grape varieties are Sylvaner, Müller-Thurgau and Riesling. Dry and fruity, these white wines are presented in the distinctive flask-shaped bottles known as "Bocksbeutel" (the design for the Portuguese Mateus Rose bottles was based on these). Like other German wine regions it is being left behind by more modern winemaking enterprises in other countries. But it's well worth trying, and if you are able, bringing back from your holiday, as it's usually quite expensive outside Germany. Federweisse appears in September, this is the freshly tapped new wine.

www.frankenwein-aktuell.de is a portal for the Franconian wine industry.

Sekt is German sparkling wine, popular for celebrations, although Prosecco, an Italian sparkling wine is currently quite a trendy drink at parties. Weinschorle is a refreshing "spritzer" of wine and mineral water.

Most pubs and restaurants also offer cheaper wines from France and Italy.

Low-alcohol and non-alcoholic drinks

Given that beer is usually very cheap, local pubs are obliged by law to offer at least one non-alcoholic drink that is cheaper than beer.

Radler (a beer and lemonade mix) can be found in most pubs and derives its name from its suitability for cyclists who don't want to fall off. It usually has an ABV of around 2.5%. British "lager top" fades into insignificance in the face of such unappealing drinks as Russiches or Russ' (Weissbier and lemonade), Spezi (cola and orangeade) and Colaweizen (cola and Weissbier)! See the website www.abseits.de/biermix.htm for an incredible selection of unpleasant-sounding beer mixes. It is reassuring to know that the dirty brown opaque liquid you occasionally see being drunk in half-litre glasses is probably one of these and not a specimen of the local beer.

Limonade is a generic word for fizzy soft drinks, not necessarily lemonade. Several breweries produce their own range of soft drinks.

Apple juice is more popular than orange and it is also served mixed with mineral water as Apfelschorle.

Mineral water (Mineralwasser) comes in still and fizzy versions – be warned that the latter – particularly those from spa sources – can have a high mineral content which may not agree with all stomachs. You may also prefer to drink still bottled water rather than tap water if only because the latter, although perfectly safe, is different in composition from your tap water at home.

Coffee is good and strong, but generally served with evaporated milk or "Kaffee-Sahne" (creamer) rather than fresh milk or cream. Some cafes now offer espresso, capuccino or filter coffee. Tea will not meet the requirements of British palates. Inevitably it will be made with water that is not quite at boiling point and will be served weak with the aforementioned Kaffee-Sahne; the alternative of lemon (often a sachet of lemon juice rather than a slice of lemon) may be a better option.

Traditional pubs (like Schlenkerla) may eschew coffee and cola drinks altogether.

A RECIPE FROM BAMBERG

Bamberger Zwiebeln (Bamberg beer onions)

Ingredients (for 4 people):

4 large (Spanish) onions.

400gm mixed minced meat (pork and beef, or pork and smoked ham)

2 eggs

1 or 2 stale bread rolls, soaked in milk and squeezed dry

Half a bunch parsley, chopped.

Salt, pepper, marjoram, nutmeg

Zest of one lemon

Tablespoon of thick cream

4 round, thick slices of smoked bacon

50cl Smoke beer or other dark lager beer

40cl Meat stock

Method:

1. Peel the onions and cut a thin slice off the root end of each onion so that it sits firmly upright.

2. Cut a slice off the top side of each onion to make a lid.

3. Hollow out the onions leaving the walls 1cm thickness and season inside with salt and pepper.

4. Finely chop the flesh scooped out of the onion and mix it with the minced meat, bread, and lemon zest. Season with nutmeg and marjoram.

5. Fill the onions with the mixture. Put the lid back on each onion.

6. Put the onions in a dish with the hot stock and bake for 75 minutes at 180° or until tender.

7. Remove the onions to a serving dish and keep hot.

8. Drain off the liquid into a saucepan and add the beer. Thicken it with potato flour or cornflour. Finally add a dash of cream.

9. Pour the sauce over the onions.

10. In the meantime fry or grill the bacon.

11. Place a bacon slice under the lid of each onion and serve with pureed or fried potatoes, or simply with sliced Franconian country bread.

Tip: given the different types of onions available in the UK, it might be useful, after hollowing them out, to parboil them before stuffing.

Travel and tourist information for Bamberg and Franconia

Tourism

Getting to Bamberg from the UK is no easier than it was 25 years ago. Over the years various operators have provided flights to Nuremberg, but both the operators and flight timetabling have changed frequently over the years, and no doubt will continue to do so. Currently Air Berlin operates daily flights from London Stansted (except for Saturdays), but they depart mid-evening which really necessitates staying overnight in Nuremberg and travelling on to Bamberg in the morning. There is also an additional outward flight on Monday mornings. Return flights are also mid-evening. Booked in advance fares are as low as £105 return (April 2009). Air Berlin **T** 0870 73 88880 **www.airberlin.com**.

As an alternative for those who do not want to travel from Stansted there are several flights from Heathrow, mainly with Lufthansa, to various German airports where you can take connecting flights to Nuremberg. Booked in advance the return flight can cost about £165 (**www.lufthansa.com T** 0845 7737747). There are also similar deals from KLM (**T** 08705 074074, **www.klm.com**), involving changing in Amsterdam.

A fly drive package would be worth considering for a group of three or four people planning to travel around Franconia. Some of the tour operators listed below provide these.

Arriving at Nuremberg you find a small, modern airport which is pleasantly un-busy, if rather short on facilities. Clearing passport control etc rarely takes long and immediately outside the airport are the steps to the U-Bahn (underground railway or subway) which will take you to the main railway station (Nuremberg Hauptbahnhof) in about 12 minutes. The ticket machine (at pavement level) has instructions in English, but you still need to take care to get an adult rather than a child ticket. The airport is the terminus of the U2 line so there is no chance of inadvertently travelling in the wrong direction!

Nuremberg Hauptbahnhof is a typically frenetic German main station, always very crowded and requires you to be rather more streetwise than is usual in this part of Germany. Trains to Bamberg run about three times an hour but one is very slow indeed taking over an hour. A frustrating experience if you are craving your first Seidla of Bamberg beer!

If you fly into Frankfurt or other German airports the onward train journey is quite long and expensive, but you should look at the various deals on the DB website (**www.bahn.de**). The journey from Munich to Bamberg is now much shorter (two hours) as a result of track improvements so this is an option worth investigating.

To travel from London to Bamberg by rail using Eurostar is now a very viable alternative to air travel. The travel time is now around nine hours now that the new fast trains from Brussels to Cologne and Aachen and the new track between Cologne and Frankfurt have improved the journey time. By taking the 08:27 Eurostar train from London St. Pancras to

Brussels you can reach Bamberg by around 18:30 local time in the evening.

Eurostar **www.eurostar.com** and Rail Europe 08705 848 848 **www.raileurope.co.uk** can book you through to German destinations including Nuremberg via Eurostar.

Bamberg is tucked well away from the areas normally favoured by British tourists in Germany, who seem to gravitate around the Rhineland and Munich. There is not much promotion of this region in Britain; I did once see a feature on Bamberg and Franconia on a British TV travel programme that must have lasted all of three minutes!

Only a few UK tour operators include Bamberg and Franconia in their itineraries. Specialist tour operators for Germany in the UK include:

DER Travel Service Ltd (DER TOUR) **T** 020 7290 1111, **www.dertour.co.uk**

German Travel Centre Ltd **T** 020 8429 2900, Fax 020 8429 4896 **www.german-travel-uk.com**

The German National Tourist Office's site **www.cometogermany.com** is aimed at the US and Canadian market and directs you to tour operators that specialise in travel to Germany.

Beer tourism

The untimely death of John White in 2007 brought an end to his "beer hunts" which introduced dozens of British beer drinkers to Bamberg and Franconian beer. However, Chris Pollard, famous for his Podge's Belgian Beer Tours, intends to include an occasional trip to Bamberg in his itineraries. **www.podgebeer.co.uk T** 01245 354677.

Bier-Mania offers "cultural beer tours" to Europe and the USA's beer zones **www.bier-mania.com**.

You can plan your own holiday and although travelling times will be of necessity long (Bamberg is 600 miles from London), once you have arrived, you benefit from cheap food, beer and accommodation. Prices are considerably lower than in Munich and other big German cities. American tourists seem to be more familiar with the area, possibly because a large number of American servicemen and women were based here.

A free set of useful pamphlets (in English) about Bamberg is published by the Bamberg Tourist Office and includes an accommodation list. In London the German National Tourist Office London offers an on-line brochure service. Contact **T** 020 7317 0908, FAX 020 7317 0917, web site **www.germany-tourism. co.uk**, EMAIL **gntolon@d-z-t.com**. The office itself is not open to the public. Information on other places in Franconia is also available.

Bamberg Tourist Office

Call in here as soon as possible after you arrive, to get information for your visit. The tourist office is situated at Geyersworthstrasse 5, D96033 Bamberg, **T** 0049 951 29 76 200, FAX 0049 951 29 76 222 or EMAIL **info@bamberg.info**.

The website is at **www.bamberg.info**. The opening hours of the tourist office are Monday to Friday 0930–1800, Saturdays 0930–1600, Sundays and holidays 0930–1430.

Besides the brochures mentioned above, there is a lot more information available here, although most of it is in German only. There are various beer-focussed guided tours available.

The "Bamberg Card" (details available in English) entitles you to take a two-hour tour of the city, travel on buses for 48 hours and admits you to six museums (including the brewery museum) and other places of interest. In 2010 this cost €9.50.

There are also some glossy guides to Bamberg available locally, and these have editions in English and other languages.

The Bamberg city website is **www. bamberg.de**.

Accommodation

Accommodation is available from about €40 per night and can be booked through the tourist office or on their website. No charge is made for this service. However not all hotels in Bamberg participate in the on-line booking scheme.

Bamberg is a popular tourist destination and in the past had a shortage of hotel beds, a situation that is now improving with the opening of several large new hotels. However it is still advisable to book in advance, particularly for the period July/August; at other times conferences may result in a shortage of hotel beds. You can of course make reservations yourself in advance; if you feel confident enough, it's quickest to telephone your booking; you can also book by FAX or E-MAIL, and most hotels understand English. The brewery guesthouses are good value and are ideal for beer lovers and in fact there is not much in the way of cheaper accommodation available anyway Fässla, Spezial and the Bamberger Weissbierhaus are within ten minutes walk of Bamberg station. If you are unable to secure accommodation in Bamberg you could consider staying in Memmelsdorf, or Bischberg which are only 15 minutes away by bus, or another local village.

An increasing amount of self-catering accommodation is available in Bamberg. Details are included in the city accommodation list.

There is a youth hostel (Jugendherberge "Wolfsschlucht") on the outskirts of the village of Bug, a couple of kilometres south of Bamberg on the left bank of the river Regnitz (bus 18). **T** 951 56002, FAX 55211, E-MAIL **jugendherberge-wolfsschlucht@dwbf.de**

The campsite (Campingplatz "Insel"), which also has an attractive location on the river, can be reached by continuing through Bug. **T** 56320, FAX 56321, **www.campinginsel.de**, E-MAIL **buero@campinginsel.de**.

Despite a post-war history of a large American military presence in Bamberg, English was not widely spoken in the city and even today some knowledge of German is definitely useful. However, young people are increasingly likely to speak English, often quite fluently. British newspapers are hard to find.

Local travel in Bamberg and Franconia

The new VGN-Plus day ticket allows unlimited travel on rail, bus services in the new region, which extends as far as Bayreuth. It includes Bamberg's buses and the S-Bahn and U-Bahn in Nuremberg. If you are going further afield by rail DB's *BAYERN-TICKET* gives very generous

discounts. Using this day ticket a group of up to five persons can travel through the whole of Bavaria for 28 euros. Individuals can travel for 20 euros (22 unless purchased from a machine) using the *BAYERN-TICKET SINGLE*. Valid from 09:00 Monday–Friday, no restriction other days and holidays.

Rail services

Besides good rail connections to the major cities of Germany, local services include frequent trains to Nuremberg, Coburg and Würzburg. German Railways (DB) 08718 80 80 66 can also book tickets for travel within Germany and rail rover tickets which are available for the whole of Germany (EuroDomino) or for selected regions (some of these can only be purchased outside Germany). See their website **www.bahn.co.uk**. Look out for the various discounts available for group travel by train in Germany. Supplements are payable on Intercity (IC) and high speed trains; you should ensure you have paid these and made a reservation before travelling on these trains.

Bus services

There are good local bus services in Bamberg although buses to certain outlying villages are infrequent and services are much reduced at weekends. The city's own bus services, which recently became part of a regional transport system – VGN – run from the bus station (ZOB) in Promenadestrasse, where you can obtain a timetable and route map. Online, they are at **www.stadtwerke-bamberg.de/ cms/OePNV/Fahrplanauskunft/Fahrplanheft/ Taschenfahrplan_2010.html**.

The integration into the regional network meant the renumbering of the Bamberg bus routes. The buses are fast and efficient, but strangely, you cannot get a bus direct from the rail station up to the cathedral area. The services cease by 20:00, but after that there is a limited service of "night" buses until 00:30.

The local bus services from Bamberg also take you outside the city limits to outlying villages such as Hallstadt, Stegaurach, Bug, Memmelsdorf, Gaustadt and Bischberg. Tickets can be bought at the ZOB, at certain bus stops and on board the bus, and unless bought from the driver, must be validated (i.e. inserted in the machine in the bus) at the start of the ride.

The regional buses run by OVF, Metzner and other companies provide connections to Bayreuth, Schesslitz and other locations and can be picked up at the railway station or at the bus station, where timetables are displayed.

Bicycle hire is an ideal way of touring the Franconian countryside, cycles can be hired at railway stations, and at various cycle shops. Cycles are a popular method of transport within Bamberg and pedestrians should be careful to avoid walking in the dedicated cycle lanes!

There are plenty of walking and cycling possibilities locally and walks and cycle paths are well signposted and detailed in several publications available from bookshops or the Tourist Office.

History and sightseeing

Bamberg's history, culture and attractions

Bamberg can claim 1000 years of documented history and in 1993 this was recognised by UNESCO, who declared it a world heritage site. Once the seat of the counts of Babbenberg, Bamberg became a Bishopric under Emperor Heinrich II (973–1024), the last of the Saxon Holy Roman Emperors. Bamberg was envisaged as a German Rome, an outpost of Catholicism, and a base for the conversion of Eastern Europe. Although Bishop Otto in particular continued this work, things didn't quite work out and later in the mediaeval era, Bamberg had troubled and unstable times. It was not until after the Thirty Years War (1619–1649) that lasting prosperity came to the city.

The catholic Prince Bishops ruled Bamberg from mediaeval times until their suppression during Napoleon's reign, at which time Bamberg became part of Bavaria. The Town Hall (Rathaus), perched on the bridge on the river, marked the division between the ecclesiastical and secular parts of Bamberg, the bishops'

town and the burghers' town. The bishops were often at odds with the citizens or burghers, who had settled in the Regnitz valley, on the island and around what is now the Grüner Markt. Later, the bishops of the Schönborn dynasty made amends by endowing the city with a wealth of baroque architecture, employing such famous architects as the Dientzenhofer brothers and Balthasar Neumann.

The cathedral or Dom, founded by Heinrich II dates from the 13th Century and follows a Romanesque form with four towers. The interior decoration is early German gothic, and includes such remarkable sculpture as the anonymous Bamberger Reiter or Bamberg Knight, the tomb of Heinrich and his queen Kunigunde by Riemenschneider, and the nativity altar by Veit Stoss.

Attached to the cathedral on its north side is the Renaissance Alte Hofhaltung. This was the Episcopal and imperial palace, and dates back to the 10th and 11th centuries. Picturesque 15th century half timbered buildings surround a courtyard (Innenhof) from where a gateway leads to further delights – a square with the mediaeval houses of the canons.

The abbey of St. Michael was also founded by Heinrich II and was rebuilt about 1121 by Bishop Otto. The church, remodelled in the 16th and 17th centuries, features a remarkable vaulted ceiling with botanical paintings. The whole hilltop complex retains its ecclesiastical ambience and there are fine views of the city.

Other churches are of equally ancient foundation and include St. Jakob (1070) and St. Gangolf (1063), which is the oldest church building in Bamberg. St. Stephan was first consecrated in 1020; the present building dates from the 17th century and is Bamberg's main Protestant church. St. Martin in the Grüner Markt was built for the Jesuits in 1686–91 by the Dientzenhofer brothers. The Obere Pfarrkirche, the upper parish church, is a massive Gothic building of 1338. The Karmeliten (Carmelite) church is another reconstruction in Baroque, but it is famous for its cloisters, which are the largest in Germany.

Opposite the cathedral is the renaissance Neue Hofhaltung or Residenz, the last residence of the Prince Bishops, built in 1599–1610 and completed in the baroque style by the Dientzenhofers in 1697–1703. The imperial apartments and the art galleries can be viewed. On its north-east side there is a rose garden terrace with views of the city and the Michaelsberg.

The Rathaus (Town hall) which spans the upper bridge dates from 1467 but was remodelled in baroque in the 18th century. The half-timbered "Hauslein" balanced on a pierhead must be the most-photographed building in Bamberg. There are fine views of the weirs on the river Regnitz, the quaint fishermen's cottages known as "Little Venice" and the old cranes on the river quay, from where cruises on the river begin.

The Hain is a large public park, which extends south of the city and is bordered by the river Regnitz. It contains the city's botanical garden. The other waterway of Bamberg is the broad Rhein–Main–Donau canal; only in 1992 was this major engineering feat, linking the North Sea and the Black Sea, finally completed.

E. T. A. Hoffmann, the romantic writer and poet lived in Bamberg – his tiny house at Schillerplatz is now a museum. In the same square is the theatre that bears his name; this was recently reconstructed.

Around Bamberg the Prince Bishops left their legacy in the form of the magnificent Weissenstein castle at Pommersfelden, and their summer palace, the Seehof, beautifully sited on a lake between Bamberg and Memmelsdorf.

Today's cultural attractions are comprehensive – there are 16 museums, including the new Holeographic museum. As in Germany generally, most museums are closed on Mondays. The world-famous Bamberg Symphony Orchestra under its British conductor Jonathan Nott is at the centre of the musical and artistic life of the city. It gives concerts at a new concert hall beside the river Regnitz.

Holiday attractions include sports facilities and several swimming pools. Children can enjoy the Kinderparadies (a "playzone" for ages 2 to 7) and the Naturkunde museum, and there are several theme parks within reach.

The Corpus Christi day procession in June (in which the Bamberg brewers take part) is just one of many religious celebrations in this devoutly catholic city. Other annual events include the Franconian wine festival in the Schloss Geyerswörth, the antiques week in July, and a variety of musical offerings. In June there is Canalissimo, a "water festival" by the Alte Kanal with food, music and plenty of beer bars. www.canalissimo.de. In 2010 the festival runs from 25 to 27 June. At Christmas time there is a traditional Christmas market in the Maxplatz, and the "crib route" takes you around the churches and other venues where elaborate models of the nativity are displayed.

The Johannisfeuer celebration observed on Midsummer Eve is of pagan origin and marks the summer solstice. Huge bonfires are lit up on the hills of Franconian Switzerland and of course there's beer and sausages to help the celebrations!

Beer events

23 April, the "day of German beer" (this was actually the day the Reinheitsgebot was enacted in 1516) is celebrated in Bamberg with a bar at the Grüner Markt where all Bamberg beers are served. In May there are the Bamberger Biertage (Bamberg beer days) celebrated at the Maxplatz where all the breweries have a stand, and there is live music. Both these events have changed in format over the years and it is worth checking to avoid disappointment.

Local holidays

1 January New Year's Day
6 January Epiphany (Heilige Drei König)
Good Friday
Easter Monday
1 May Labour Day
Ascension Day (Christi Himmelfahrt)
Whit Monday
Corpus Christi
Assumption (Maria Himmelfahrt)
3 October Germany Day of Unity
1 November All Saints Day (Allerheiligen)
17 November Repentance Day. This is not an
    official holiday, but schools are closed.
25 December Christmas Day (Weinachtstag)
26 December St. Stephen's Day

If the non-moveable holidays fall at a weekend, a public holiday on a working day is not designated in lieu, unlike in the UK.

Kirchweih (Kerwa)

Beer takes an important role in local parish festivals (Kirchweih, or in local dialect, Kerwa). One of the biggest is Bamberg's Sandkerwa in August. Sandkerwa to Bamberg is like "Carnival" is to Notting Hill. It takes place over five days at the end of August, however as the 2010 event is the 60th it will be extended to 7 days – 18 August to 24 August. These parish festivals celebrate the saint's day of the local church with a fair accompanied by plenty to eat and drink, and take place in the open air. The church here is the little St. Elisabeth in the Sand, the district at the foot of the hill below Bamberg's Cathedral and the other magnificent historic buildings of the "Bishop's town". Its main thoroughfare, Sandstrasse, is closed to traffic during Sandkerwa, although cele-brations also extend outside this area down to the riverside where the traditional jousting by boatmen on the river can be watched. There are other traditional set pieces like the "Hahnenschlag", the raising of the tree and the fireworks display. There are side-shows and funfairs for kids and plenty of live music, but the essence of Sandkerwa is the opportunity for Bamberg people to get together, meet old friends and stroll around the streets, eating and drinking as they go. If you're not an itiner-ant drinker, there's plenty of scope to sit down as not only do the many local bars, cafes, hotels and restaurants maximise their outdoor drinking space, but benches and tables are set up to provide temporary drinking space in the street, in business premises and in courtyards – every possible nook and cranny is utilised. A phenomenal amount of beer is consumed!

Kerwa dates

Sandkerwa: last weekend in August, Thursday through Monday. www.sandkerwa.de
Wunderburg Kerwa: third week in July, Wednesday through Monday.
Laurenzikerwa: four days ending on the second Sunday in August.
Gaustadt: first weekend in October.
Bischberg: first weekend in September.
Gartenstadt Kerwa (East Bamberg): 1st Sunday in August.

Other information for visitors

Twin towns: Bamberg is twinned with the borough of Bedford in the UK, a productive and flourishing relationship that has been in place for over 30 years. The Bedford Bamberg Association (BBA) was founded 25 years ago and has about 90 members. Although clubs and schools had exchange arrangements with Bamberg for many years, many Bedford people felt the need to form friendships on a family basis with people in Bamberg and that is how the BBA came into existence. *Contact*: Rosemary Adams **T** 01525 862 297 E-MAIL bba@bedfordbamberg.org.uk.

The Americans in Bamberg: In the closing weeks of the Second World War, American troops occupied Bamberg. This was the start of a long-standing American military presence in Bamberg. This continued through the Cold War period, as a result of the strategic position of the city near the borders with the then East Germany and Czechoslovakia. A large American community is still based at the Warner barracks.

Tourist guide books

For a good general tourist guide to the area, "Germany – the Rough Guide" was probably the best guide to Germany – it also had accur-ate and gaff-free coverage of beer and beer-related issues. It contains plenty of useful information and tips on travelling and holiday-making in Germany generally. Unfortunately the latest edition (2009) does not match the erudition of its predecessor.

The Michelin Tourist (green) Guide is useful although it majors on architecture. The guides from Fodor, Lonely Planet and the AA do not in all honesty cover the region in much detail.

Learning German and local *Dialekt*

If you want to learn German in the congenial surroundings of old Bamberg, the Treffpunkt Language Institute may be able to meet your needs: www.learn-german.com.

Dialekt. Those who struggle with the German language will probably be reluctant to explore the local dialect – in its written version it is quite daunting with its fearsome array of jagged consonants and a liberal sprinkling of Umlauts. But many dialect words are used locally, particularly the ending –la which replaces the usual German –en as a diminutive.

Lieselotte Tomaschek's book *Bamberg Dialekt in German and English* (new edition 2004) is an introduction to *Dialekt* with translations of many words and phrases into "Hochdeutsch" and English.

Bibliography and further reading

Good Beer Guide Germany, STEVE THOMAS, (CAMRA Books 2006). A directory of all German breweries with details of output, beers brewed and main outlets for each brewery. Very useful particularly for opening hours and public transport. A pity Franconia is not separated out from the rest of Bavaria in the text. The guide is updated at www.german-breweries.com.

Brewery Trail, DIETER MORCINEK, is a small booklet about Bamberg breweries, published by the Bamberg Tourist Office a few years ago (English).

Die wahre Haupstadt des Bieres, CHRISTIAN FIEDLER (2005). Magnificent account of Bamberg's breweries, past and present, great illustrations. German language only.

Brauns Brauerei Atlas, BORIS BRAUN, (Hans Carl 2003/2004). Two books that provide good and mostly up-to-date information on Franconian breweries and pubs (German language only). A new edition is awaited.

Michael Jackson's Pocket Beer Book, (Mitchell Beazley, 2000). A must for anyone interested in exploring world beers.

Prost! The Story of German Beer, HORST D. DORNBUSCH (Syris Books USA 1997), is an excellent history of brewing and beer culture in Germany detailing how today's beer styles have evolved. The author is now a microbrewer in the USA.

Biergarten – wanderungen in Franken, HELMUT HERRMANN (Heinrichs Verlag 2003), details 20 walks taking in pubs and beer Kellers and gardens.

Private Brauereigasthöfe A useful booklet containing details of 40 plus home brew pubs (most of them with accommodation) in Germany is published annually and is available free from Private Brauereigasthöfe, Hauptstrasse 19, 96117 Memmelsdorf, Germany. You can usually find copies at some of the subscribing pubs e.g. Spezial and Keesmann in Bamberg.

Die Biere Deutschlands, HÖLLHUBER and KAUL, (Verlag Hans Karl, Nürnberg, 1988), is a comprehensive, independent guide to the beers of Germany covering the major brewing styles and a region-by-region guide to breweries. It contains a great deal of valuable information on social trends in beer drinking and the survival of small breweries and traditional beers. It is a rare example of a German book on beer that is written from the consumer point of view.

Wanderführer für Biertrinker, HÖLLHUBER and KAUL, (Verlag Hans Karl, Nürnberg, 1984), These five books detail walks taking in small breweries in various regions – the Fränkische Schweiz, and the Frankenalb are the subject of two of the books, and two feature areas of Upper Bavaria. The remaining book, published more recently in 1996 is "Bamberger Bier und Aischgründer Karpfen" and covers the area lying to the south east of Bamberg, between the Regnitz and the Steigerwald. A new edition of the Fränkische Schweiz book appeared in 2004.

Die neue Fränkische Brauereikarte, STEFAN MACK, (Verlag Stefan Mack, Nürnberg, 1996), used to provide a definitive guide to the brewing scene in Franconia, and included a map of Franconia with all the breweries shown. Unfortunately although a new edition was promised, it never appeared. Stefan Mack also published guides to beergardens in various regions of Franconia including *"Keller und Biergärten von Bamberg bis Forchheim und drumrum"* 1999, and, with Arno Klinner, *"Biergärten in der Fränkischen Schweiz"* 1995 and *"Biergärten im Fränkischen Seenland und in Altmühltal"* 1996.

Kellerführer, PETER SEM, (4th Edition, Bamberg, 1994/5) is a guide to beer gardens in and around Bamberg. Kellerfuhrer II is a companion volume to the author's earlier publication and covers the Erlangen and Forchheim areas. The author has also published a guide to Kellers in Franconian Switzerland. Peter Sem is another author whose books have not been updated into new editions.

Selige Bierreise, VICTOR ZOBEL, is a new edition with modern photographs to illustrate this classic 1941 account of the author's "blissful beer travel" around Bamberg. Apart from the illustrations, the book is of academic interest only, being very hard going even if your German is good!

Die letzten 100 Brauereien in Bamberg und seinem Landkreis, UTO DÜTHORN, extols the local brewing tradition with plenty of colour photos and anecdotes, but again, rather hard going. An English language version was published more recently.

Bambergs Brauereien – Biervielfalt erleben & geniessen, is a useful little booklet about local beer styles, breweries etc, mirroring information on the www.bierstadt.de website.

Websites

www.**bierregion-franken.info**. Frank Wetzel's labour of love – a directory of virtually all Franconian breweries (around 270 of them) up to date in 2010. The listings include opening times.

www.**whitebeertravels.co.uk**. White Beer Travels. The late John White's comprehensive website about European beer is maintained as a memorial to him.

www.**bamberg-guide.de**. Local site with extensive "Bierkultur" coverage. German language only.

www.**bier-keller.de**. Vast amounts of information about Keller culture, listings of Kellers and a chance to vote for your "Keller of the year" (German only).

www.**bierstadt.de**. Links to all the Bamberg breweries' websites.

www.**beerguide.de**. English language guide to beer and breweries in South West Germany.

www.**bamberger-bier.de**. Official site for Christian Fiedler's history of Bamberg breweries.

www.**bambergbeerguide.com** or www.**franconiabeerguide.com**. Fantastic American site with a "virtual Stammtisch" where you can exchange information on beer topics concerning Bamberg and Franconia. The place to keep up-to-date!

www.**bierland-oberfranken.de** or www.**bierfranken.de**. The website of the Fränkischen Bierstrasse e.V., an association of breweries promoting beer tourism in five regions of Franconia. German only.

www.**biershop-bamberg.de**. On-line beershop.

Use of the Web and e-mail are not as highly developed in this region as elsewhere in Europe. Many businesses stick to the "Telefax" for electronic communication. Most breweries and pubs now have websites, and there are a number of sites of interest to the beer lover with some knowledge of German. However not all are well maintained and many links will be found to be missing.

Appendices

Appendix 1
German beer

Germany is one of the world's greatest beer drinking nations, in fact it can be rightly claimed that beer is the national drink. The tradition goes back to mediaeval times when the beer purity law of Bavaria set a standard that is maintained and revered to this day. In the 19th century German brewers took a lead in developing lager beers, a type of beer which now accounts for most of the world's output.

Germany still had over 1290 breweries in 2001, a total that had increased slightly over the previous six years. This increase was due to new microbreweries opening and disguises the ongoing closures of small and medium size breweries. The number of breweries in Bavaria declined from 714 to 654 in this period. Overall output of beer across Germany has remained static over the last ten years. Consumption per head has declined from 141 litres per head per annum in 1970 to an estimated 123 in 2001 (Source: Deutscher Brauer-Bund). Consumption per head is much higher in Bavaria and even higher in Bamberg.

The Reinheitsgebot or beer purity law was issued on April 23 in the year 1516 and stipulated that beer could only be made from barley, hops and water. It initially applied only to Bavaria but gradually was adopted throughout Germany, and by 1906 was official law in the whole of imperial Germany. By then yeast had been added to the basic permitted ingredients and wheat allowed as an ingredient of top-fermenting beers. In 1987 the EEC ruled that the Reinheitsgebot was a restraint of trade.

Since then it has been legal to import beers that do not conform to the Reinheitsgebot into Germany and for German brewers to brew non-Reinheitsgebot beer – although Bavarian brewers stick strictly to the Reinheitsgebot.

A facsimile of the original beer purity law (Reinheitsgebot) issued in 1516.

Appendix 2
The malting and brewing process

A step by step guide to the production of beer in Germany, giving the location of each part of the process.

Maltings (Mälzerei)

1st STEP: **Steeping** *(Weichen)*

First the barley has to be soaked in water in order to start the germination process. In the language of brewers this is called "steeping". During this process, the grain is alternately steeped and aerated.

2nd STEP: **Germination** *(Keimen)*

After the water content in the grain has reached 35%, it starts to germinate. When the grain begins to grow, enzymes are formed, which are able to break down the contents of the grain (mainly protein and starch) later on in the brewing process. During the 7-day germination period the "green" malt is constantly turned and aerated.

3rd STEP: **Kilning** *(Darren)*

In order to stop germination and to stabilise the involved biochemical processes, the green malt must be dried – this is normally carried out in gas-fired kilns. To produce smokebeer (Rauchbier), a beechwood-log fire underneath the kiln heats the air, and the smoke gives the malt its typical flavour.

Breweries without their own malthouse – the vast majority – can purchase different types of malt from commercial maltings. For them the brewing process starts with Step 4.

Brewhouse (Sudhaus)

4th STEP: **Grinding** *(Schroten)*

To continue the transformation process started in the malthouse, the malt must initially be crushed into grist.

5th STEP: **Mashing** *(Maischen)*

The grist is mixed with water in the mash tun. In the resulting mash, the enzymes can convert the components of the malt. The most important step is the transformation of starch into malt sugars. (n.b. local breweries may use either an infusion or a decoction mash.)

6th STEP: **Wort Separation** or **Lautering** *(Läutern)*

After the conversion process is finished, the sugar-rich malt liquid, the wort, is separated from the solid components, the spent grain. The wort is then transferred to the brew kettle, while the spent grain is removed from the brewery, and can be used, for example, for baking bread.

7th STEP: **Boiling** *(Kochen)*

The wort is boiled in the kettle and the hops are added in several stages. Through the heat the bittering elements in the hops are released, giving the beer its distinctive bitterness. During the boil, water evaporates so that the wort reaches the necessary concentration (original gravity). Some components of the wort become insoluble through the heat; these substances are called the "hot break" and must be removed subsequently. The overall process in the brewhouse from mashing to the completion of the boil takes about 8 hours.

8th STEP: *Cooling and Pitching* (Kühlen und "anstellen")

After boiling, the wort is pumped into the whirlpool and the wort is "drawn off". Here the hot break is removed. Subsequently the wort is cooled (to 5 Celsius for bottom fermenting beers, 15 Celsius for top-fermenting beers) aerated and the yeast is "pitched".

Fermentation room (Gärkeller)

9th STEP: *Primary Fermentation (Hauptgären)*

In this process, malt sugar is converted into alcohol and carbon dioxide.

At the end of primary fermentation, which lasts approximately 7 days, most of the yeast settles to the bottom of the fermenting tank. For this reason, it is called bottom-fermented beer. The yeast in top-fermented beer e.g. wheat beers, rises to the top of the fermenting tank. The "green" beer is now pumped to the lagering cellar for secondary fermentation.

Lagering cellar (Lagerkeller)

10th STEP: *Secondary Fermentation and Maturation (Nachgären und Reifen)*

Now follows a period of maturation to perfect the beer. The remaining fermentable elements in the green beer are transformed by the yeast, whereby more carbon dioxide is created. The conditioning/storage tanks are closed with a prime regulator (a pressure release valve) which is set to a specific counter-pressure.

In this way the carbon dioxide content in the final beer is regulated. Maturation takes between 4–8 weeks at 0–1 Celsius, after which the beer is ready to drink.

(Wheat beers only spend a week in the lagering tanks and complete their maturation in the bottle or cask, at a temperature of around 6 Celsius.)

11th STEP: *Filtration (Filtrieren)*

At the end of the secondary fermentation, the beer still contains yeast and other suspended matter. The majority of beers are filtered in order to give them clarity. After that, they can be filled into either kegs or bottles. In some breweries the filtered beers may be held in tanks prior to filling or may be dispensed straight from the tank.

Bottling and racking (Abfüllen)

After thorough cleaning and inspection, the casks and kegs are filled under counterpressure. Through pre-pressurisation the beer flows into the casks and kegs without foaming. Similarly, the bottles are filled under counterpressure and are subsequently labelled and packaged.

With acknowledgements to Heller-Bräu Trum (Schlenkerla)

Useful German pub and brewing terms

Ausleger Hanging sign of a pub

Bernstein Amber (colour)

Bierfilz, Bierdeckel Beer mat

Bierkeller or **Sommerkeller** *see chapter 4*

Bierkieser A beer taster, similar to a British aleconner.

Brauerei Brewery, hence Brauereigaststätte or Brauereigasthof (pub belonging to a brewery), Brauerei-Ausschank (brewery tap or tied outlet), Hausbrauerei (brewpub). Many pubs are still signed Brauereigastätte even though they have not brewed for years – as is the case with French brasseries. The sense of the word "Brauerei" is closer to "brewing company" rather than the physical buildings which may be referred to as Brauereistätte.

Brennerei Distillery.

Bügelflaschen Flip-top bottles.

Dunkel Dark, hence "dunkles Bier". Anything but the palest colour beer is considered a "dunkles Bier" in Germany, but Bernstein is sometimes used for an amber coloured beer.

Fass Barrel (GB) or Keg (USA)

Fassbier. Draught beer.

Flaschenbier (fl.) Bottled beer.

Hefe Yeast.

Heimdienst Home delivery service.

Hell Light (in colour). Used to denote a pale-coloured beer, hence "helles Bier".

Hopfen Hops.

Kasten Case or crate (of bottled beer)

Kneipe Small pub or bar.

Lagerbier Beer that has been stored or lagered.

Leicht. Light (in alcohol).

Malz. Malt.

Mälzerei Maltings.

Nebenzimmer An additional guest room or bar, used when the main bar is full.

Obergärig Top-fermented. Such beers are in the minority in Germany but include Weissbier, the Altbier of Dusseldorf and the Rhine Valley, and Kölsch, which is native to Cologne. Unlike in Britain, the distinction between top and bottom fermented beer is featured in advertisements, although the significance to the consumer is uncertain.

Pfand Deposit (on bottles, cases, casks, mugs etc).

Reinheitsgebot The Bavarian beer purity law, dating back to 1516 and stipulating that beer can only be brewed from malt, hops, yeast and water.

Schenke In traditional Bamberg brewpubs, a serving hatch used for takeouts and by those drinking in the courtyard.

Selbsabholer Take out service, offered by most small breweries in the form of bottled and cask beer. Bought by the case (Kasten, 20 bottles) beer is usually extremely good value by British standards e.g. around 40p for a 50cl bottle.

Siphon. A 2 or 3 litre glass bottle with a flip-top stopper, sometimes used for takeouts.

Stammtisch Table reserved for the regulars in a pub.

Sudhaus In a brewery, this is where the mash and the boiling of the wort take place.

Ungespundenes Now usually called Ungespundetes. Franconian beer speciality which is vented to the atmosphere during lagering and has low carbonation.

Untergärig Bottom-fermented. Most German beers are of the "lager" type and are fermented with bottom-fermented yeast. Whilst in Britain such beers are almost always of the pilsener type, there are many styles of lager beer in Germany and these are not exclusively pale in colour.

Vollbier "Full" beer, a generic name for the standard beer of about 5% ABV.

Vom Fass (v.f.) Draught, i.e. from the barrel or keg (Holzfass denotes a wooden barrel).

Wirtshaus/Wirtschaft An old name for a pub.

Appendix 4
Bamberg beer chart

BREWERY	BEER	ABV	NOTES
Ambräusianum	Hell	N/A	
	Dunkel	N/A	
	Bernsteinwerizen	N/A	Amber wheat beer
	Doppelbock	N/A	Seasonal (November)
Fässla	Gold Pils	5.5	
	Lagerbier	5.5	
	Zwergla	6.0	Märzen
	Weizla	5.0	Wheat beer – pale and dark
	Bambergator	8.5	Seasonal Doppelbock
Greifenklau	Lagerbier	4.8	
	Bock	7.0	Pale seasonal Bock
	Weizen	5.2	Wheat beer
Kaiserdom	Premium Pils (Extra Dry)	4.9	
	Alt-Bamberg Dunkel	5.2	Dark lager
	Meranier	5.2	Black lager
	Weizenland	5.3	Wheat beer – pale, dark, Kristall
Keesmann	Herren-Pils	4.6	
	Helles	4.5	
	Sternla	5.0	Unfiltered Lagerbier
	Bock	6.2	Seasonal pale Bock
	Weissbier	4.8	Wheat Beer

NOTES: 1. Principal beers only are listed, not the complete brewery range.
2. Alcohol-free and low-alcohol beers are not listed.
3. ABVS of beers are as supplied by the breweries, and may change from time to time.

BREWERY	BEER	ABV	NOTES
Klosterbräu	Gold Pils	5.0	
	Schwärzla	4.9	Black lager
	Braunbier	5.7	
	Bockbier	7.0	Seasonal pale Bock
	Schwärzla-Bock	7.0	Seasonal dark Bock
	Maibock	7.0	Bock for May
	Braun's Weisse	4.9	Wheat beer
Mahrs	Helles	4.9	
	Pilsner	4.9	
	Ungespundete Lagerbier	5.2	Known as "U"
	Bock-Bier	6.5	Seasonal pale Bock
	Weisse Bock	7.2	Lenten dark wheat Bock
	Mahrs-Weisse	4.9	Wheat beer
	Gig	5.2	Märzen
Schlenkerla	Aecht Schlenkerla Rauchbier	5.1	Smoke beer, Märzen strength
	Ur-Bock	6.5	Seasonal smoke beer
	Helles Lagerbier	4.3	Not a smoke beer
	Fastenbier	5.5	Lenten beer
	Weizen	5.2	Wheat beer with smoked malt
	Eiche	8.0	Christmas Doppelbock
Spezial	Lagerbier	4.5	Smoke beer
	Märzen	5.3	Smoke beer
	Ungespundetes		Not a smoke beer
	Weizen	5.3	Wheat beer with smoked malt
	Bock	6.9	Seasonal smoke beer

Maps

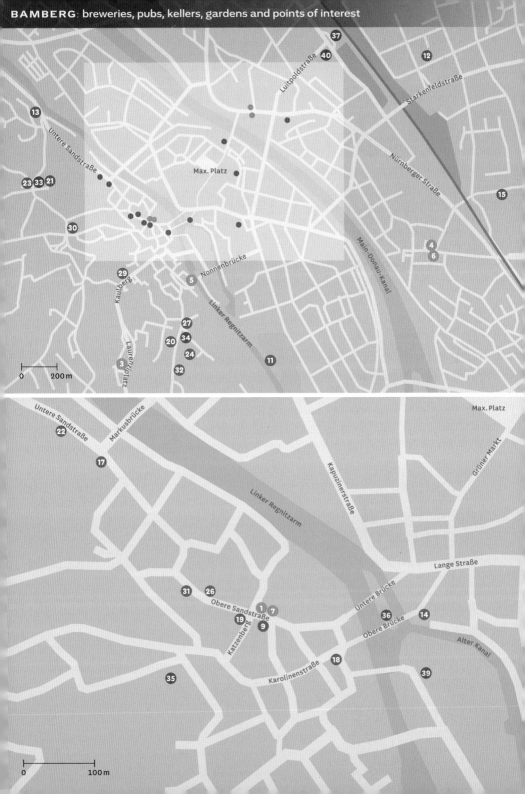

BAMBERG: breweries, pubs, kellers, gardens and points of interest

Breweries

1. Ambräusianum
2. Fässla
3. Greifenklau
4. Keesmann
5. Klosterbräu
6. Mahr's Bräu
7. Schlenkerla
8. Spezial

Pubs, kellers and gardens

9. Alt-Ringlein
10. Bamberger Weißbierhaus
11. Bootshaus
12. Café Abseits
13. Englischer Garten "Zum Bockser"
14. Eulenspiegel
15. Fässla-Keller
16. Fässla-Stub'n
17. Griesgarten
18. Hofbräu
19. Kachelhofen
20. Mahr's Keller
21. Michaelsberg Café & Restaurant
22. Pelikan
23. Schmitt's Café
24. Spezial Keller
25. Sternla
26. Stilbruch
27. Stöhrenkeller
28. Tambosi
29. Tapas-Bar
30. Torchuster
31. Weinstube Pizzini
32. Wilde Rose Keller

Points of interest

33. Franconian Brewery Museum
34. Brauerei Heller-Trum
35. Bamberger Dom (Cathedral)
36. Altes Rathaus (Old Town Hall)
37. Bamberg Railway Station
38. Central Bus Terminal (ZOB)
39. Tourist Office
40. Post Office
41. Post Office

BREWING TOWNS AROUND BAMBERG

HASSBERGE

Baunach

Kemmern

73

Dörfleins

70 E48

Hallstadt

70 E48

73

26

Weiher

STEIGERWALD

Bischberg

Gaustadt

Bamberg

Trabelsdorf

Mühlendorf

Stegaurach

Bug

Debring

22

22

Untergreuth

Reundorf

Mönchsambach

22

Herrnsdorf

505

505

Greuth

0   1 km

Würgau

Scheßlitz

Merkendorf

Drosendorf

70 · E48

Memmelsdorf

Schammelsdorf

Huppendorf

Tiefenellern

73

F R Ä N K I S C H E

Geisfeld

Roßdorf a. Forst

S C H W E I Z

73

Strullendorf

505

Hirschaid

Gunzendorf

Buttenheim

Drügendorf

Schlammersdorf

Eggolsheim

Schnaid

Hallendorf

Kreuzbergkeller

Stiebarlimbach

Unterzaunsbach

Forchheim

Indexes